Making Sense of the
MADNESS
An FASD Survival Guide

JEFF NOBLE
of FASDFOREVER.COM
and TARA SOUCIE, BA, BSW

Copyright © 2012 Noble Initiatives

All rights reserved.

The information contained in this guide is for informational purposes only.

I am not a Medical Doctor, Psychologist, Psychiatrist, Social Worker or Lawyer. Any legal or parenting advice that I give is my opinion based on my own experience. You should always seek the advice of a professional before acting on something that I have published or recommended. Any amount of results disclosed in this guide should not be considered average. The material in this guide may include information, products or services by third parties. Third Party Materials comprise of the products and opinions expressed by their owners. As such, I do not assume responsibility or liability for any Third Party material or opinions.

The publication of such Third Party Materials does not constitute my guarantee of any information, instruction, opinion, products or services contained within the Third Party Material. The use of recommended Third Party Material does not guarantee any success. Publication of such Third Party Material is simply a recommendation and an expression of my own opinion of that material. No part of this publication shall be reproduced, transmitted, or sold in whole or in part in any form, without the prior written consent of the author. All trademarks and registered trademarks appearing in this guide are the property of their respective owners.

Users of this guide are advised to do their own due diligence when it comes to making decisions and all information, products, services that have been provided should be independently verified by your own qualified professionals. By reading this guide, you agree that myself and my company are not responsible for the success or failure of your decisions relating to any information presented in this guide.

MAKING SENSE OF THE MADNESS

This book is dedicated to my beautiful partner, Tara. Without you, there would never have even been page 1.

And to all of you who deal with Fetal Alcohol everyday, whether you are living with it, or caring for someone living with it. My hat goes off to you. You have the hardest job in the world.

Jeff Noble | fasdforever.com

MAKING SENSE OF THE MADNESS

FASD has changed my life.

You are probably reading this E-Book because we connected somehow through my website, Facebook page or it's been passed on to you by a family member of friend. Either way, I'm really glad you are here. I'm a pretty excited guy by nature, but I am most excited to share with you everything I know about Fetal Alcohol Spectrum Disorder (FASD). I really believe this information will help you have more good days then bad. And man oh man, I had my share of bad days when I too, was a primary caregiver. In fact, as a foster parent I was fed-up, overweight and massively overwhelmed. If I didn't get answers soon, I was going to have to quit and carry the shame and guilt of letting myself down, but more importantly, failing a young man who would be off to yet another placement.

Deep down inside I knew there had to be another way...and I was right. I had been to trainings in the past and read a bunch of stuff online, but I often found the information to confusing and full of information that only doctors would understand. It wasn't until I went to a training by Donna Debolt, did I have my Aha! moment and quickly began using what I learned to create many successful living environments for people living with FASD. In fact, it has become my passion and mission to help people realize these kids aren't bad – they are just misunderstood. And I want to help you understand.

I wrote this guide in hopes it would do just that - GUIDE you. I hope it gives you some idea on what to do next. You are the expert on your kids. I am merely here to share my testimony with you about what I lived through and what I learnt about. I really do believe this is the hardest disability to deal with. My goal is that you come out the other end with a better idea of what folks living with FASD are going through and why they act the way they do. I want to help you try and make sense of the madness that is Fetal Alcohol Spectrum Disorder. It is not only until we truly understand, can we then make successful accommodations.

If this book helps just one person, then it is worth all the negatives I had to go through to get it published. Just remember you are strong, you can do this!

Jeff Noble

Join the conversation! You can find me on Twitter @JeffNoble or on Facebook at facebook.com/fetalalcoholforever.
If you prefer email, write to jeff@fasdforever.com.

Looking forward to hearing from you!

Jeff Noble | fasdforever.com

MAKING SENSE OF THE MADNESS

WHAT YOU NEED TO KNOW

What is FASD Anyways?   7
Primary Characteristics
Secondary Characteristics
Tertiary Characteristics
CNS and Sensory Issues
Executive Functioning

A New Way of Thinking   27
Grief & Loss
Paradigm Shift
Creating New Hopes and Dreams

Your 'A' Game   45
Knowing When and Why You Are Burnt Out
You're #1!

Behind the Scenes   61
Getting a Diagnosis
Assessments
Finding Their Strengths
Getting Organized

The Art of Sales   83
The Sales Pitch
Building Your Sales Team
Buying In

Your Ticket to Success   101
What Works
What DOESN'T Work

Jeff Noble | fasdforever.com

MAKING SENSE OF THE MADNESS

WHAT IS FASD ANYWAYS?

Primary Characteristics	11
Secondary Characteristics	17
Tertiary Characteristics	19
CNS and Sensory Issues	20
Executive Functioning	22

Jeff Noble | fasdforever.com

WHAT IS FASD ANYWAYS?

Fetal Alcohol Spectrum Disorder, or FASD, is an umbrella term that describes the range of effects that may occur to an individual whose mother drank alcohol during her pregnancy. These effects may include physical, mental, behavioral, and/or learning disabilities with possible lifelong implications. Some babies are born with severe physical differences and intellectual disabilities; others are only slightly affected (Streissguth, 1997).

I know we see this definition everywhere, but what does it even mean? Let's try and break it down.

FASD is a lifelong, permanent brain based disability. Also referred to as organic brain damage – meaning it's natural, it was damaged at birth and will continue to develop with damage. There is no cure. In fact, prenatal exposure to alcohol is linked to 60 health related issues. Read more about that at www.faslink.org/ResultsPrenatalAlcohol.htm.

This happens when an expecting mother drinks alcohol anytime during her pregnancy - from day 0 to 9 months. What this means is, that there is no safe amount of alcohol to drink while someone is pregnant. Anyone who says otherwise is wrong. I say this, because it is SCIENCE. The Surgeon General also maintains that "there is no safe amount of alcohol, or a level of alcohol below which there are no effects. Between 50%-70% of all pregnancies are unplanned, and social drinking prior to knowledge of pregnancy is common (Riley, 2003).

The point of this book however, is not to convince you that Fetal Alcohol exists, but rather to help you as a caregiver, to make sense of this disability.

So, is FASD the actual diagnosis?

Nope. Don't forget - it's an umbrella term. However, there are four commonly used diagnoses: FAS, pFAS, ARND and SE. This is how I remember the difference between the diagnoses:

Fetal Alcohol Spectrum Disorder (FAS)
All of the face characteristics and all of the brain damage.

Partial Fetal Alcohol Syndrome (pFAS)
Some of the facial features and all of the brain damage. This is what one of my guys was faced with and at first I thought 'partial' meant only a little bit. Let me remind you - this is not the case. There is no such thing as a little bit.

Alcohol Related Neurodevelopmental Disorder (ARND)
None of the facial features, but all of the brain damage. Ninety percent of people living with FASD are diagnosed with ARND. That's why it is so hard to wrap your head around the disability – those effected don't often 'look' effected.

Alcohol Related Neurodevelopmental Disorder (ARND)   Fetal Alcohol Syndrome (FAS)   Partial Fetal Alcohol Syndrome (pFAS)

Primary Characteristics

Primary characteristics are what comes with the package - the direct result of drinking during pregnancy. Now, we have to remember that not every kid is the same or has these same challenges, so I am going to list what I think are the more common (and challenging) primary characterizes of those with FASD.

Learning Difficulties
Encarta Dictionary states that the definition of 'learning' is "the acquisition of knowledge and skill". Because FASD is permanent brain damage, those with FASD, have trouble with learning and holding on to the information. We learn, so we can grow and adapt to our environment, but for this group – easier said then done.

Poor Short Term Memory
Does it seem like the person you know living with Fetal Alcohol forgets appointments or what you said, oh, five minutes ago? That's probably because they have seriously short term memory. Please remember, this is not their fault - it's part of the package. Also, if they are having a tough time as a young person, they will likely have a hard time as an adult too.

Inferior Auditory Memory
So what happens to them is that when you ask them to clean their room, take out the garbage and do their homework, they may only remember <u>one</u> of those instructions. This will also most likely stay with them for the duration of their stay here on earth.

Delayed Auditory Processing
Not only do they have a hard time with memory and remembering steps, but they also take longer to process what you say. So, you may be speaking at your normal pace but they only hear every other or every third word.

Impulsivity
This is why so many of these kids are labeled ADD or ADHD. Because they don't have the part in their brain (or it is damaged) to make them stop and think about what they are doing – the frontal lobe. They act first and act questions later. They are not doing this on purpose - this is part of their disability.

Abstract Concepts

This one is a biggie. People living with Fetal Alcohol often can't see or understand anything that's not concrete. Which by definition, is exactly what an abstract concept is. These are things that we can not see, so for example, money is an abstract concept. Not the actual money itself, but the day to day value - what we get from money. So, that's why people living with Fetal Alcohol are horrible with their money, which makes it hard to pay bills when their older.

Time is also abstract. For most people, we have a sense of the time. We have an internal clock that tells us when to eat, sleep, etc. Folks with FASD are often missing that cue. That's why they are often late. If I told my foster guy to be ready in five minutes, I might as well tell him to be ready by November, because they have no idea most of the time.

> So, think about this – most people are supposed to make their <u>money</u> last a certain amount of <u>time</u>, but how are you expected to do that on your own, when your brain wasn't built with the tools to do so?

Developmental Dysmaturity

People living with FASD often act their shoe size not their age. Diane Malbin explains it perfectly - "Dysmaturity is different from immaturity. While immaturity suggests the person could function in a manner compatible with age, dysmaturity means the person is functioning at a level younger than their chronological age. So, what that means is that someone who is 16 years old may act more like 8 years old and someone who is 30, may act like they are 15. The point here is that they are not acting like this on purpose, they actually can't function at the level of their chronological age. Does that sound like any of your guys?

This is also why they often get along with people younger then them - people who are closer to their developmental age. You can remember what developmental age is by asking yourself, 'how old do they really act?" It's stage - not age.

Problems with Attention

As a person living with ADHD, I can tell you from first hand experience what this is like. No matter how hard you try or no matter what you say to yourself, you just can't control it. I remember telling myself at the start of a new semester in high school, 'Ok Jeff, this is it. You are going to pay attention and do better in school'. Twenty minutes later I am either standing in the hall or sitting in the principal's office. I used to sit in class when everyone was doing work and envy them.

Honestly. I wanted so badly to pay attention to my work, but before I knew it I was daydreaming about that week's hockey game or what was going to happen on the next episode of wrestling.

In order to learn something we have to pay attention, so it was really hard for me to do both. Now, can you imagine what someone with FASD goes through when they are trying to learn and they can't even sit for five minutes (and in school they are expected to sit for the duration of the entire class...Yeah freaking right)?

So, because of their inability to pay attention they are often diagnosed with ADD, but as we continue to learn they have a lot more going against them then just paying attention.

Judgment

Contrary to popular belief, people with FASD do not make poor decisions on purpose. They make poor decisions because that part of their brain was affected by alcohol - the frontal lobe. Mary Berube says this about judgment, "judgment means you can sort out whether this was a good idea or a bad idea before hand."

So, if we know now that this is what comes with the package can you see why folks with FASD have difficulty in social situations? Isn't a large part of life judging whether things are a good idea or bad idea? I mean, even with good judgment we can sometimes mess up and make a bad decision. The difference is we have the ability to reflect on that decision and know it was a bad one - then go on to say we are never, ever going to do that again and for the most part, we don't.

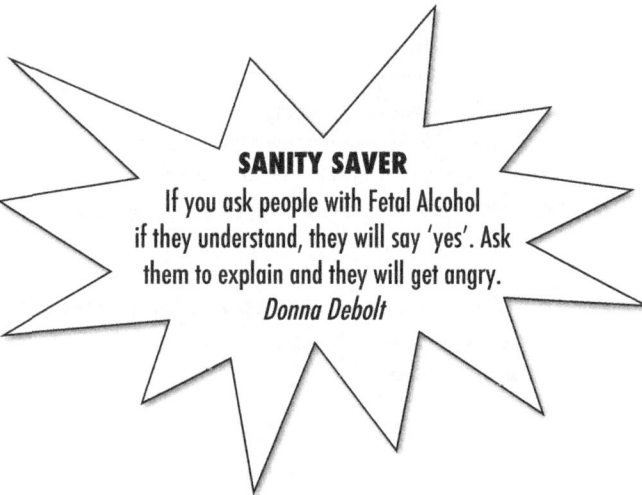

SANITY SAVER
If you ask people with Fetal Alcohol if they understand, they will say 'yes'. Ask them to explain and they will get angry.
Donna Debolt

Natural or Logical Consequences
Often times, people living with Fetal Alcohol have a very difficult time knowing what will happen next, so when they do make poor decisions, they don't know that there will be consequences. Even when it happens again and again (and again) they seem blown away by what always happens next - like it was the first time they did it.

So, a logical consequence would be if I don't save my money I can't pay my rent, and if I can't pay my rent, I will get kicked out. The person with FASD can not understand that they will likely lose their housing, which is an actual truth for many folks.

So, I think you are probably starting to understand why some of our folks act the way they do. And why they can easily get into trouble at home, work, school and even with the justice system. We expect them to behave a certain way, yet they really don't have the tools required. And when we get frustrated as caregivers, we assume that these kids are being called what Dan Dubovsky calls NURMU®.

MAKING SENSE OF THE MADNESS

Non-compliant Uncooperative Resistant Manipulative Unmotivated Without understanding that their behaviour is a result of their organic brain damage, we as caregivers try and change the behaviour the way our parents, teachers, family members and society have done for years.

We try and modify that behaviour or teach them a lesson by:
- grounding
- lecturing
- yelling
- giving them extra work
- time outs
- loss of privileges (which means taking away things that they actually enjoy in hopes of teaching them a lesson)
- more chores
- peer pressure

And hey, when those don't work we tend to step it up a bit by:
- shaming them (What's wrong with you? How can someone act like this?)
- isolate them
- physically abuse them
- suspend them or even expel them
- send them to jail

And at the end of the day, when all of those things don't work we throw our hands in the air and say they are just 'bad' people.

So, let's imagine how it must feel to be in trouble everyday for things you can't control, but everyone thinks you can, and you are just choosing not to. And the worst - you aren't able to defend yourself because you don't have the skills to do so.

How frustrating would it be if every time you looked into someone's eyes all you seen back was that 'look' of disappointment? Even though you tried so, so, so hard to do well and all you wanted to do was to have people be proud of you.

What happens when you get so frustrated with a problem and everyone around you seems to be 'getting it', but you just can't figure it out? What happens when you try to do something for what feels like one thousand times and fail one thousand times and get one thousand reminders of that failure?

You experience, what is referred to as a secondary characteristic.

Secondary Characteristics

Secondary Characteristics are a result of <u>chronic</u> frustration, trauma and failure that happens again and again and again. For the most part, these behaviours are a <u>normal protective response</u> to the massive amount of pain people living with FASD face everyday. It's also been described by Diane Malbin as a, "poor fit between the needs of the person and their environment". Basically, they are tired of trying because they are sick of failing.

If you can remember anything about secondary characteristics, remember this - they can be prevented. Secondary characteristics develop over time because these folks become frustrated, sad and quite simply, pissed off because they don't know what's wrong and either does anyone else. There are many secondary characteristics that people with FASD are affected by, here are a few of the more common and challenging that you will likely see:

SANITY SAVER
FASD is like an iceberg; most of the problems are hidden from view.

Mental Health Diagnosis
In a study by Streissguth, it was established that 90% of people living with FASD have mental health problems often diagnosed with anxiety, depression and/or PTSD. In fact, a few videos I watched more recently mentioned that some are beginning to believe that since it is such a high percentage that a mental health diagnosis may be a primary characteristic.

Easily Frustrated
An everyday annoyance may seem like the end of the world to those with FASD.

Often times when you try and help, it only sets them off further which could lead to one hot mess.

Aggressive
Like in-your-face aggressive or even physically aggressive.

Anxious
I know of one young man that was so anxious that the only thing he could tolerate besides his house was a ride in the car. I had made attempts to have him enter a public place and forget about it! If you have ever had an anxiety attack you know how much they suck and sometimes seem like it is the end of the world. Well this is sometimes a daily reality for folks with FASD.

Quick to Fatigue
Because these kids are 10 second kids in a 1 second world and they often have difficulties with sleep, they can get tired really quick. We get cranky and irritable when we are tired, well so do they - it just happens a lot faster and a heck of a lot more often.

Poor Scholastic Performance
They are horrible in school. It's a sad reality, but it is a reality. Multitasking is not one of their best skills, so listening, writing, staying still, and being mindful of the time in a place where they are probably feeling overly stimulated, is likely a recipe for disaster.

Over or Under Active
It can look a stray bullet bouncing around a room like you see in the movies or the exact opposite - saying nothing and do nothing and no matter what you say or say you are going to do, it does not matter! They just shut you off. This could probably make you so frustrated you could scream or cry or both. I know! Been there.

Tertiary Characteristics

Tertiary Characteristics happen when those with FASD fall through the cracks - when all of their supports give up and everything starts to fall apart around them.

These include:
- constantly in trouble at home, school or in the community
- constantly running away from home/placements - often referred to as awoling
- females are at a higher risk of unplanned pregnancies
- in and out of custody
- homelessness
- substance use/abuse
- gangs

I think we can agree, tertiary characteristics are basically every parent's worst nightmare that just doesn't seem to end.

Jeff Noble | fasdforever.com

CNS and Sensory Issues

Ok. So far so good, right? I realize I have been putting a lot of emphasis explaining the connection between alcohol exposure in utero and the brain, however what a lot of people forget or don't know is that alcohol not only attacks the brain, but the central nervous system (CNS) as well. The effect of alcohol on the CNS causes people living with Fetal Alcohol all kinds of trouble.

Our central nervous system takes in information through our senses - touch, smell, hearing, seeing and taste - and organizes them in the brain.

Most of us do not need to worry about that because our brain filters the information on its own. If by chance our brain can't sort out the various senses, it will get overwhelmed and give us a cue. From there, we can make adjustments to the environment. For example, if you walk into a room and the lights are too bright, what do you do? You turn the light off or down. What happens if the room is too hot? You can go and adjust the thermostat. TV too loud? You get yelled at by your partner to turn it down (Or is that just me?)

Now - if you want to do an experiment at home to see what if feels like to be someone living with this disability here is how you do it.

Step 1 Put on your favourite wool sweater

Step 2 Turn up your room temp up 30c

Step 3 Sit on the hardest chair you have in the house

Step 4 Turn your radio up a little too loud

Step 5 Have someone stand across the room preferably under a bright light

Step 6 Have that someone read from a text book

Step 7 Sit there for 60 minutes

Bonus Have the person at the front of the room give you looks and constantly ask you to sit quiet

What did you think about that? If you had a hard time with that, it's because your senses were overloaded causing you to become overwhelmed which almost always turns into anger and then the grand finale, a meltdown.

I remember when one of my guys was not having a particularly good day in school and on the way home I had asked him if anything was too bright or too loud. He had said he started to get frustrated during group work because "EVERYBODY WAS MAKING @#$%ING NOISE!" I then asked him to tell me what it feels like and he said, "It feels like I am playing Guitar Hero on Expert and the notes are coming at me sooooo fast."

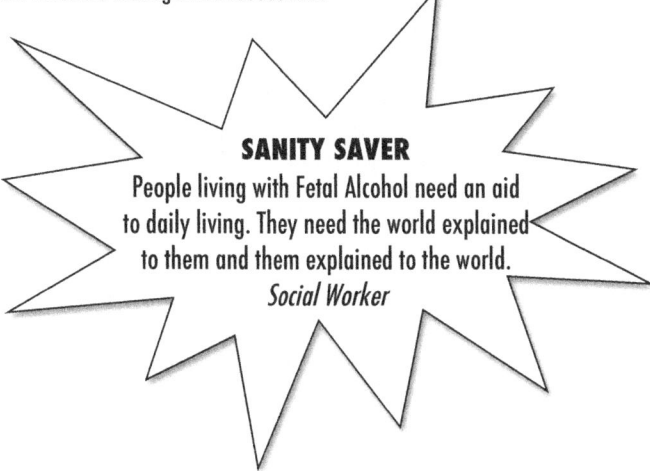

SANITY SAVER
People living with Fetal Alcohol need an aid to daily living. They need the world explained to them and them explained to the world.
Social Worker

People living with Fetal Alcohol may be **Hyper Sensitive**, which means they are super duper sensitive. Even the slightest touch on their skin might feel like a slap. I know a lot of folks who had to have tags removed from their clothes because they bugged him so much. On the other hand, some people are what's called, **Hypo Sensitive**, which means they have a difficult time feeling anything at all.

I'll never forget when I first saw my foster guy wear shorts in the Winter!!! I couldn't believe it. When I first seen this I thought, 'Honestly?!' But, he swore up and down that he wasn't cold. Another young man I know would squeeze his game controller so hard you could see white knuckles. He told me he couldn't feel the controller. So, as caregivers it's important to keep this in mind - that it is both the brain and the body that are damaged by alcohol.

Jeff Noble | fasdforever.com

Executive Functioning

This is when things started to turn around for me. This is where I really started to understand what this disability was all about. I can't remember if it was one of her trainings, classes, consultations or conversations, but I'll never forget when Donna Debolt said this - "If you have good executive functioning that means you're a good grown up." People living with Fetal Alcohol have poor executive functioning and that's what gets them into trouble as they get older. I can remember Donna bringing this up over and over again when sitting in on her consultations. Everybody assumes that if you have a high enough IQ then you must be smart enough to complete the tasks expected of you.

Well, that's not always the case. Your IQ is <u>what you know</u> and your executive functioning is <u>what you do with it</u>. So, it's one thing to know something and it's another thing to do something with that knowledge. Let's take a look at what's involved in executive functioning.

Your executive functioning is controlled by the frontal lobe of your brain. I've heard executive functioning described as a conductor in an orchestra or the traffic cop of the brain. Executive functioning is responsible for a number of very important day to day tasks. If someone has poor executive functioning, which those with FASD do, a simple task turns into a real hot mess.

Planning and Organizing

For most of us, we have the ability to plan and structure most of our day. First we have to make the plans and then we have to pull it together to make sure it happens. Remember elementary school? Teachers generally planned everything – from when to eat, when to go out, when to speak, when to listen, when to pee, etc. But what happens as these elementary students turn into middle school students and high school students?

Teachers and supports around them do less planning and organizing for the students because they are expected to be able to carry out tasks and instructions on their own. Well, if a person's ability to plan and organize is blunted, it is going to make navigating through life a really tough experience. So, imagine what it feels like to have everyone telling you that you can do something and that you must be lazy if you are not.

Getting Things Started (Initiating)
That's why they talk about doing a lot of things, but never do. For example, how many times have you heard, 'I'm moving out' or 'I'm getting my license'. They know what they want, but just CAN'T get started.

Following Through
This is when they say they are going to do something but are unable to do it. I learned very early on to not make plans with my guy and expect him to remember and follow through, because it just wouldn't happen. But, often folks get into trouble because it seems like they are doing it on purpose (not following though) when in fact, they forgot or were unable to follow through.

> **People living with FASD act first, then process the information later.**
>
> **The brain of someone with FASD is usually ten minutes behind everything else.**
>
> **By the time they realize what they have done, it's too late.**
>
> **That's impulsivity...and not their fault.**

Regulating Emotion
Regulating your emotion means you are able to tolerate frustrations and it gives you the ability to think before acting or speaking. I bet there are days where all you do is tolerate people (and their silly ideas) and the reason you don't freak out and speak your mind is your ability to self regulate. People living with Fetal Alcohol in some cases, do not. So, that's why they say what they want to say when they want to say it.

Executive functioning also controls our internal dialogue as well. You know when your guys do something for the hundredth time and you are so mad but you are able to talk yourself out of a brain haemorrhage with a little self talk.

Like this - 'Calm down Jeff...it's not his fault, he didn't mean to do that. It's not the end of the world.' If we didn't have that ability to self talk to calm ourselves down, we would just blow our tops off all the time. People living with FASD may not have this skill and because of that, it can seem like they can go from 0 to 60 super fast.

Managing and Setting Goals

We all know in order to be successful you have to set goals. Then when you are done setting the goals the next step is to manage the goals through measuring progress and revaluating. That takes significant functioning to do that. People living with this disability often can't do this. This inability will often get them into trouble and is also extremely frustrating for these guys to have to go through.

Ability to Shift or Adjust your Thinking

We do this one without thinking. We are able to move from one situation, activity or problem with little effort. Some of my guys just couldn't shift from one problem to the next. For example, I remember when one of my guys wanted to do something and there was NO WAY and I mean NO WAY it could happen. He just wasn't able to shift or transition to another topic - he couldn't let go or move on from what he wanted to do, even though there was no way it could happen. This is also referred to as perseveration. Another guy had the toughest time moving onto dinner, even when it was ready, smelling delicious and on the dinner table. It was always the same – he would be watching TV or participating in some sort of activity, everyone would run when the sweet chime of 'dinner's ready', but not this guy. It wasn't because he was being defiant he just needed help shifting from one activity to the next.

Stopping or Inhibiting

We have all been victims of an impulse purchase or made a decision a little too quickly. We have all had moments where at the time something seems like a good idea (or better yet when we are mad there are things we would like to do to people) however, we have the ability to not act on every little impulse. Life is full of those moments when we need to 'hit the brakes'.

People living with Fetal Alcohol don't have any 'breaks' and that causes all kinds of problems. Sometimes my guy would do something and later on, when we would debrief, he would say he just didn't know why he did things he literally did just moments before. What they need is to always have someone in the passenger seat with them - like a driving instructor that also has a break on their side.

So, ask yourself does IQ matter? You could the have the highest IQ in the world but nothing can be done with it if you don't have good executive functioning. <u>People with Fetal Alcohol have horrible executive functioning</u>.

Think about where that leaves them when they reach adulthood and are expected to maintain housing and employment. And this will hopefully give you a better idea as to why many adults with FASD are either homeless, unemployed or both. I know this may look like I am painting a bleak picture...and in a way I am. I need people to understand that people with this disability are often a lot less capable in some area's then we think, even though they look and sound so 'with it' sometime.

Jeff Noble | fasdforever.com

MAKING SENSE OF THE MADNESS

A NEW WAY OF THINKING

Grief & Loss	29
Paradigm Shift	38
Creating New Hopes and Dreams	41

A NEW WAY OF THINKING

A great teacher, Donna Debolt, once said, "we have to give up what we thought it was going to be like and take on what it really is."

Grief & Loss

It is assumed that we only experience grief and loss when we lose a loved one or a treasured pet, however a very key step in becoming an equipped FASD caregiver is accepting and being a part of the process of grief and loss. Embracing grief and loss is one of the most crucial elements in becoming a successful caregiver and sadly, it is often the most overlooked and under serviced area of FASD care giving.

Let's face it - this is not what you had in mind. But, wait! There is hope! I'm going to share with you what I have both lived and learned about grief and loss, because one thing I know for sure is, if we aren't able to deal with the matter, we will not be able to move forward.

Caregivers like you experience more loss then most families and unfortunately, it will likely be an ongoing challenge. So, why exactly do we call what we are experiencing grief and loss? Well, being the caregiver of someone with irreversible organic brain damage forces you to shift your thinking, change your old methods, parenting techniques and approach – the act of grieving what you 'thought' raising your child was going to be like. You will have to develop new ideas, parenting strategies and hopes and dreams. Your ability to accept these differences and new challenges will allow you to move on and truly enjoy your loved one.

In **Dan Dubovsky's** video (visit www.fasd.alberta.ca), he discusses family and loss. I think he's bang on, do you?

Loss of Hopes and Dreams
Everyone has hopes and dreams. As humans, we have aspirations to succeed and this is true for caregivers as well – whether you are an adoptive parent, foster parent, family member, etc. Before you became a caregiver I bet you pictured something very different - Easier? Less frustrating? More sleep?

When what we thought was going to happen, doesn't happen, and hopes and dreams of caregivers aren't met - that's a loss. Is this true for you? Does it make you angry or sad when you see that things aren't turning out the way that you would have liked them to? If this has been your experience, don't worry, you are not alone.

Loss of Family and Social Support
Friends don't come over nearly as much, if they even come over at all. They don't want to hear about what is 'really' going on. Some of you may not have as much family support as your child grows older and their behaviours continue to escalate. Even worse, it's difficult to share your true feelings in fear of sounding looking like a bad caregiver. That's a huge loss and it is certainly ok to think about and even be sad about.

Siblings
They wanted a sibling to play and share experiences with - now they have to deal with the behaviours and may possibly have to take care of the disabled child when they are older. They may become resentful towards the person with FASD if they do not understand that the behaviours and outbursts are not the fault of the person with FASD.

Loss of Financial Means
There is a reason they call people living with FASD million dollar babies. They are expensive because they demand so many resources and you will likely experience financial loss, inability to save any money and in most cases, money is super tight to begin with. That's a loss - does it make you mad? Or maybe even resentful?

Loss of Companionship
You lose the connection with your partner because you are focused on the current disaster or you are constantly waiting for the next one. If you are not arguing about money, you might be arguing about what to do next. I know - I've been there.

> **When I was a foster parent, my relationship with Tara was definitely at odds. If I wasn't arguing with Tara I was arguing with our foster kid because he needed that much attention.**

There is very little time to put energy into your relationship with your partner, so they often fail. That's why there is such a high divorce rate among couples raising someone with a disability.

Loss of Ability to Revel
One of the best parts of being a parent are the times you get to revel and enjoy the accomplishments of your child. I don't have any biological children but I still do understand what that means. There is nothing better than basking in what your loved one has accomplished. Not being able to do that is a loss. And one that is really tough to embrace.

Loss of Self Esteem and Competence
Whether you are a foster parent or a biological parent, how good you are as a parent is reflected in how good your kids are. So, if your kid is constantly

misbehaving you are likely seen as a 'bad parent'. I can remember my parents watching the news when I was younger and hearing the latest news reports about some crime committed by a younger person, they would say, "What's wrong with those parents? That boy needs a good, swift kick in the behind. That's all they need."

I believe what really happens is that parents like yourself are doing your very best and the person living with FASD is still acting up. But people will continue to point the finger at you as part of the problem. The same thing happens with professionals. Some of them will talk nice to you, but when you leave they still think you are part of the issue - seems like you can't win sometimes.

That's a loss. Everyone, and I mean everyone, wants to seem competent. So, when your looked at like your not doing a good job it hurts your self esteem and competence.

I don't remember where I heard this from – I think it was from a caregiver, and she said that it feels like your going to get fired every day. That's a loss, and not to mention a terrible feeling.

It happened to me when I was having a particularly hard time with one of my guys. No matter what I did he was still getting into trouble at home and in the community he was totally out of control. By this time I thought I had a particularly good knack for dealing with these kids and more importantly stabilizing them – but no matter how hard I tried, he just didn't seem to get better.

I had to write a bunch of incident reports to my agency which turned into a bunch of meetings. I knew they looked at me as part of the problem. My stomach was in serious knots all the time! I had lost all my confidence as a caregiver and most times, I'm a pretty confident guy. My self esteem was in the dumps and it felt horrible to be looked at like I wasn't good enough. That was a loss that I had experienced and it was not fun.

MAKING SENSE OF THE MADNESS

So, now it is your turn.

I want you to do an exercise that will help you with the process of Grief and Loss.

Write down all of the 'losses' that you experience as an FASD caregiver. The reason I am asking you to do this is because we have to recognize what our losses are before we can move on from them.

Dan Debovsky says that if we don't acknowledge the loss, we will hold on to it and because of that, we will never be able to move on. We will always be living in a state of loss. Are you not tired of living like that?

Complete the exercise on the following page.

EXERCISE

What are the 'losses that you and your family have experiences?

_____
_____
_____
_____
_____

What feelings do you have about your family's loss?

_____
_____
_____
_____
_____

What did you think it was going to be like raising your child?

_____
_____
_____
_____
_____

What is raising your child really like?

_____
_____
_____
_____
_____

Now, I'm not trying to be a Debbie Downer, but if we're looking at the losses that we face, we must also recognize that those with FASD experience loss as well. They may not be able to explain to you what they are feeling, but you will likely see their feelings through their actions.

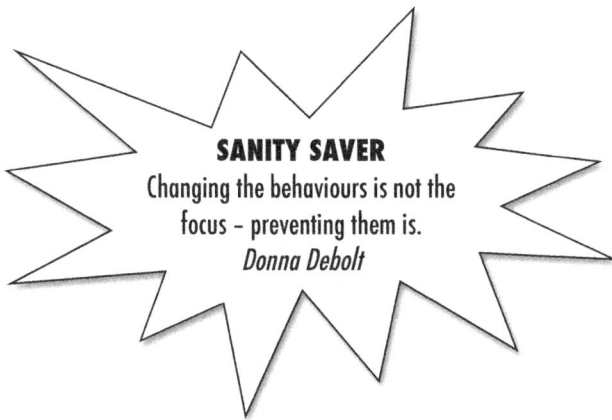

SANITY SAVER
Changing the behaviours is not the focus – preventing them is.
Donna Debolt

Hopes and Dreams
Just like us, people living with FASD have hopes and dreams, too. They get sad when their hopes and dreams aren't being realized; and often other people will tell someone with FASD that they can't do things. I've heard it with my own ears. We have to make sure we are doing our best to nurture their dreams, even if some of their expectations may seem above their capacities. For example, if they say they want to be a doctor, don't tell them they can't be a doctor. To them, working at a hospital might be just as good as being a doctor.

In some way, this is still helping them realize there dream. And at the very least, we want them to feel supported and like their dreams are important too. Who wants to feel like they have limited possibilities for their future? NO ONE. Including these guys.

Loss of Milestones
Don't think for one second that they don't see what other kids are doing at their age. Because of their developmental delays, they are unable to hit many milestones at the same time as their peers and guess what? That's a loss.

One of my guys used to ask me why he hadn't graduated high school yet like other people. Or why didn't he have a car like other people his age? My natural tendency would have been to blow it off and say something like, 'oh no, you're on your way too, buddy' in hopes of blowing off a possible freak out. But, after watching Dan Dubovsky's video (visit www.fasd.alberta.ca) where he said that it was ok to recognize their losses with them and that it was ok to talk about it, my new approach was to acknowledge his feelings and ask him more questions. But, what did he say after I asked him what his thoughts were? Something along the lines of, 'ya, I don't think that's fair, but that's ok. I am going to get my license for monster truck's first'. Seriously.

Loss of Family Stability
For some of these kids they have been through so many placements they feel a loss of stability. Imagine how you would feel if you have had to live with dozens of other families only to get kicked out for behaviours that are out of your control. Ouch. Believe it or not, I have met kids who have been in more than fifty placements!

Try to see it this way - look beyond the behaviours as bad and start looking at the behaviours as losses. Here is a good example about an amazing young man I have had the pleasure of spending a lot of time with. He has an IQ of 52, which is pretty low. His sister lives in a very rural community in Northern Ontario. She comes for visits a few times a year around the holidays at which time she is accompanied by her social worker. Although the visits have always been positive, after she leaves, about a day later, his behaviour changes. Because he wasn't able to process his feelings of sadness and loneliness, he acted out. After talking to him about this, we realized he was experiencing the loss of his family member and also experiencing memories of where he also once lived with his sister.

I know another young lady that always acted out more then usual around the same time every August. She would act more moody, less compliant and she would get into trouble in the community. People were focusing on her behaviour and not looking at the big picture. What could she be acting out for? What is she trying to say? We found out later on that her father's birthday was around the same time. Coincidence? I didn't think so.

What do we do about it and how do we move on?

Here's what needs to happen in order to let go and move on from these losses. We need to talk about the reality of the losses and accept them as such. Recognize that these are real and painful. Really recognize that your loved one won't be doing things at the same time as their peers. Come to realize that, you might not have financial security like other families do. So, if you are a family or are working with a family, it's really important to remember to recognize how much pain that causes so again we can believe it and move on. Because only when that happens we can address the issues and take the time to regroup and reorganize. When this happens, you will start to notice a change in direction of how you handle your loved one and what your expectations of their goals are, which over time, will bring you more good days then bad.

Jeff Noble | fasdforever.com

Paradigm Shift

Things won't change for someone living with Fetal Alcohol until we change the way we think. Hopefully by now you have a better understanding of what FASD is and what causes these guys to act the way they do. I also hope that you have begun to seriously see this as a time to grieve about it since you have to begin taking on what it really is. A part of doing so, is to shift your thinking from thinking that someone with FASD is doing things on purpose, that they are bad and don't care about anything. That really is the farthest from the truth. People living with this disability want a normal life, just like you and me - the problem is that they were not born with the tools to allow them to do it unsupported.

The real magic happens when we shift our thinking from they WON'T do something to they CAN'T do something. I know that even when we do this, it's still so hard not to take it personal. I assure you this is nothing personal and that their behaviour is brain based not character based.

If you're having a hard time wrapping your head around this one, I get it.

The Paradigm Shift (shifting your thinking) really is one of the hardest lessons you will learn as an FASD caregiver. Diane Malbin explains it nicely with the following diagram. Check it out. Print it out and put it somewhere where you can see it everyday. It will really help when you feel like you are about to lose your marbles.

Diane Malbin says, "As our understanding of the meaning 'organic brain differences' is integrated into every life, at home and in the community, parents and caregivers undergo a personal and professional paradigm shift in how they understand and feel about children with FASD. This shift includes moving from:

From seeing person with FASD as:	**To understand person with FSAD as one who:**
Won't	Can't
Bad	Frustrated, defended, challenged
Lazy	Tries hard
Lies	Confabulates; fills in
Doesn't try	Tired of failing; exhausted; can't start
Mean	Defensive, hurt, abused
Doesn't care; shut down	Can't identify or show feelings
Refuses to sit still	Overstimulated
Fussy; demanding	Oversensitive
Resisting	Doesn't "get it"
Trying to make me mad	Can't remember
Trying to get attention	Needs contact; support
Acting younger	Is developmentally younger
Thief	Doesn't understand ownership
Inappropriate	May not understand proprieties
Not getting the obvious	Needs to be retaught many times

Once I was able to get a grasp on this, my whole world changed. Not only was I starting to look at my foster kid differently, I started to see everyone differently. I also began to feel guilty because I realized my expectations of him where unrealistic. I assumed just because he looked like he was fifteen and sounded fifteen, that he was capable.

Don't get me wrong, it takes a long time to be able to do this automatically, but the fact that you're even open to the idea that these kids aren't bad they are just incredibly damaged and misunderstood puts you ahead of the game. But, don't forget to keep this page handy, because it's easy to slip back into old habits and find yourself frustrated all over again. Especially when you find yourself looking at someone who is a specific age and isn't able to live up to the standards, even though sometimes they do.

Creating New Hopes and Dreams

Everything is not lost. Once we get a better understanding that this disability is permanent brain damage and that these folks' futures may not look like we had first thought or planned, certainly does not mean that they can't have one. Quite the opposite. I have seen people in this population be very successful - we just have to change our definition of success.

Remember - in order to create new hopes and dreams we must let go of the past. We have to do our best to realize that none of this was anyone's fault. This includes your loved one for being born this way and for everyone else who doesn't really understand about the situation.

> **Just because someone living with Fetal Alcohol can't be an Astronaut doesn't mean they can't work for NASA.**
>
> **Just because your kid will never become a doctor doesn't mean he will never be able to work at a hospital.**
>
> **Just because your kid will never play in the 'big leagues' doesn't mean they won't be able to work in professional sports.**
>
> **Just because someone living with Fetal Alcohol may never get married they can still find love.**

Start thinking it's possible
The agency I worked at would get the worst of the worst. Kids who had been kicked out of every group home and agency in the province it seemed like. Often times they were being placed with my agency or headed to jail. My point

is, that we have been able to turn some of these really crappy situations around. It's possible. We have to be able to help these folks create new hopes and dreams, and in doing so, we must also create new hopes and dreams for ourselves and our families.

Knowing what you know now about FASD and everything that goes along with it, what would some new hopes and dreams be for your family?

What are YOUR new hopes and dreams?

MAKING SENSE OF THE MADNESS

YOUR 'A' GAME

Knowing When and
Why You Are Burnt Out 49

You're #1! 53

YOUR 'A' GAME

Being a caregiver to someone with FASD is like sitting in the back seat. You are always, always and always putting other people first. Well, the truth of it is, you have to put yourself first. So, move over and get behind the steering wheel!

I can say without a doubt caring for someone living with Fetal Alcohol was the most difficult thing I have ever done in my entire life. PERIOD! It is the most lonely and emotionally exhausting task I have ever undertaken. Not to mention, it's a job that everyone else thinks your horrible at, people often reflect your parenting skills based on your child's bad behaviours and you probably feel alone most of the time. Well, it's no wonder you forget to take care of yourself. But, I'm here to remind you that be a kick ass caregiver, you have to put yourself first, too.

By the time I was done foster parenting I was about 40 lbs overweight and had an issue with anxiety. The mere thought of having to deal with my guy would leave me with knots in my stomach - not because I hated the guy but the fact that he required so much care and sometimes I just didn't have the energy to invest that he required. You know as well as I do, that if you don't have enough energy, that might be the difference between a good day and a really bad one.

Being a caregiver to someone with this disability is so hard. I have known some caregivers who suffer from severe depression and post traumatic stress disorder. Yikes!!

I also remember being in a state of confusion from time to time. I was always second guessing myself. It was so hard to know if his behaviours were a result of his FASD or was he just being a brat? The truth is, it was like I was just barely keeping my head above water - until I learned through trainings, conferences and a bunch of different video's that what I was feeling was super typical.

Knowing When and Why You Are Burnt Out

This is the key to your personal resurrection. I have been burnt out twice during my time as a primary caregiver. Once with my foster guy and the other not too recently during this past summer. If you subscribe to my newsletter's you may remember as my experience has been very well documented. It wasn't until my foster kids adoptive Mom mentioned something to me that made me realize that I was, done like dinner. His mom had a very big part in his life, which was awesome for us because she would take him every second weekend, which gave me some relief. She is an incredibly strong woman and a big reason why I started this endeavour in the first place.

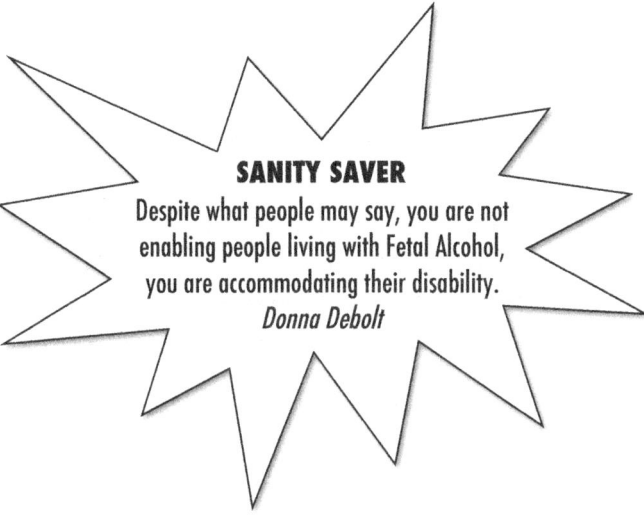

SANITY SAVER
Despite what people may say, you are not enabling people living with Fetal Alcohol, you are accommodating their disability.
Donna Debolt

I will always remember when she looked at me and said, "I know that face, Jeff - You are burnt out." Of course I said 'no'. I wasn't going to admit it. But, I knew she was right. I was suffering from compassion fatigue. I sank into my chair and started to cry. And that's when I stopped being in denial.

In her book, <u>Fetal Alcohol Spectrum Disorders: A Collection of Information for Parents and Professionals</u>, Diane Malbin lists some of the characteristics of caregiver burnout.

Do you experience any of these? I bet you do.

- gradual onset
- self depletion
- exhaustion of one's physical and mental resources
- wearing oneself out be excessively striving to reach some unrealistic expectation imposed by one's self or by others
- discrepancy between intellect and emotion
- prolonged discomfort, including anger and fear
- continuing to strive to reach unrealistic expectations without articulating or modifying these expectations
- overworking, taking work home
- increased frustration, decreased tolerance
- preoccupation, detachment, boredom, cynicism,
- feeling unappreciated: anger and resentments "flare"
- relationship/communication/sexual/intimacy problems
- denial, other defenses (e.g. under- or oversleeping)
- diminished sense of self esteem
- paranoia, disorientation, physical complaints
- depression, denial of feelings, gradual reduction of outside interests

So, if you can identify with some or all of these characteristics, let's take a look at maybe why this has happened.

Let's start off with Diane Malbin's explanation - "people with FASD and their families and parents, as well as the professionals who work with them, often experience the effects of burnout. Chronic failures associated with the discrepancy between the perceived ability of the individuals living with FASD and their actual ability or performance creates burnout. Becoming burned out is a process. Recovering emotional resiliency takes time."

MAKING SENSE OF THE MADNESS

Let me show you what the difference between what our expectations are of someone with FASD and what their performance/ability/outcomes really look's like:

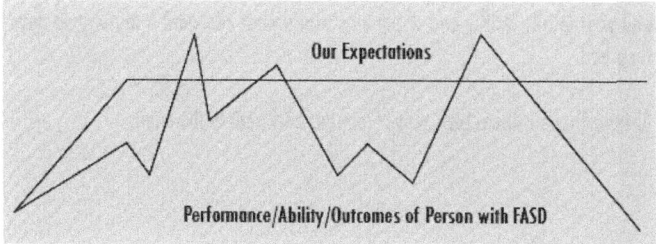

Adopted from Diane Malbin

Now, let's break that down a little further. Our expectations of our guys are too high. Burnout happens over time.

> **We don't experience burn out because those with FASD couldn't perform what we expect just once – we experience burnout from feeling let down and disappointed by them over and over again.**

The big kicker here and what tends to drive us batty, is that sometimes they meet or even surpass our expectations, so we think they get it and that they have learned the new skill or ability, and then we expect that they will be able to do it over and over again.

WHO WOULDN'T GO CRAZY!

It's really difficult as a caregiver to want so badly for your child to succeed, but when they don't and they crash, we take it personally or we get angry because we think they did it on purpose.

The truth is, your loved one who is living with FASD will crash again. But, what you must remember is that the more you learn about FASD, your ongoing commitment to your health and practicing good interventions, the more likely it is that you will see compliant behaviours which results in better days for you and your family. At the end of the day, that's what you want - more good days then bad.

Alright. That's it then. Let's move from the back seat to the front.

You're #1!

Yes, you are! And you have to be at your best when dealing and living with someone who has FASD. Here are the strategies that I have used to keep my spirits up, my confidence high and keep away burn out.

Change your Expectations
The brain of a person who is living with Fetal Alcohols is like that light bulb in your house with a short in it. Sometimes it works perfectly and shines all day other days it flickers on and off. Then there are those days when no matter what you do, the light is not coming on. Realizing this will allow you to react with appropriate interventions and save you a boat load of stress.

Knowing your Triggers
We have to know and recognize what pisses us off, what our pet peeves are. If we can figure that out, then we can identify when someone squeezes the trigger. It will help us to understand that we are not really mad at the person living with Fetal Alcohol, but instead, they just hit one of our triggers. Knowing this, we can rebound from the situation a lot quicker and not have a bigger problem.

Pick your Battles! AKA Don't Sweat the Small Stuff
This is one lesson that has really helped me. If there is one thing that I know about people living with Fetal Alcohol is that you can't convince them their thinking is off, because their thinking is off. So, when any of my guys ask me to do anything, I ask myself – 'will this hurt them, me or anybody else?' If no, then 'no worries'.

Remember, they live in the present and can't see some of the consequences that may lie ahead. This is why some of their questions seem bizarre to us. These guys just can't anticipate anything going wrong with their plans. So, if their request is something that I would like to disagree with, I would negotiate the outcome that I wanted for this particular request.

That way, they still get a little bit of what they want and you can avoid a possible meltdown by having to say no. And, of course, redirect them after that and move on!

Take Time to Nurture your Other Relationships

Since these guys do take up so much time and emotion, make sure you find the opportunity to spend quality time with your other kids and your partner. This is a must. As we know, spending quality time with your family will recharge your batteries and will give you a chance to distress about issues occurring in your home. It's ok to have some time with your family without the person living with Fetal Alcohol. It's respite and it's encouraged.

Vent

Things can get pretty frustrating caring for someone with FASD and keeping your frustrations bottled up inside is not good for anyone. What happens is, even though you are not saying your frustrated you will certainly have a frustrated energy about you, which people living with Fetal Alcohol can pick up on.

Having someone you can vent to will be very helpful. But remind that person that you are just wanting to vent and not necessarily looking for answers. The last thing you want when you are trying to deal with a bad day is someone telling you what you 'should' have done. If you don't have someone that can provide you that type of support, consider a support group. If neither option is for you, e-mail me Jeff@fasdforever.com. I'm serious. My website has been up for a few years now and I get a couple of these types of emails a week. If that's the only outlet you have right now, then please write me. It will make you feel a heck of a lot better. I promise.

DO NOT and I Repeat DO NOT Compare Yourself to Other Caregivers

Don't even compare yourself to other FASD caregivers. Trust me. Everyone has their own issues to deal with and no two people living with Fetal Alcohol are the same. Comparing will only bring about negative feelings which, without knowing it, you will pass onto your family. If you must compare yourself, watch an episode of Springer. That'll make you feel better.

Learn to say NO!!!

Stop trying to be a superhero! Your loved one requires a lot of your energy. So, when someone asks you to help them out doing this or that, tell them you will get back to them in a couple of days. If you still feel like you want to do it, you'll feel good about the decision and have no problem fulfilling your commitment. Often times, we spread ourselves too thin trying to make up for the shortfalls of the person with FASD. My problem was I would always give everyone a ride, which often took me from my work. Then, when I did finally did have time to myself or with Tara, I usually had to leave again to go pick that person up. People won't be angry if you say 'no' to their requests, and if they are then too bad for them - your sanity is on the line.

Go for a Walk
I can't tell you how many times this kept me from losing my stuff! If you're able to go out for a walk when you get upset, just leave and go for a walk. Not only is it good for your health, but it's a fantastic way to blow off steam. Usually I spend the first 5 minutes of my walk cursing under my breath, then as I burn off the negative energy I am able to remind myself that this person has organic brain damage. I remind myself not to take it personally.

SANITY SAVER
Sometimes as caregivers we have to talk less, so our kids living with Fetal Alcohol can understand more. Keep explanations sunny and short.
Donna Debolt

The last 5 minutes of my walk I spend trying to come up with a solution. What I found was that when I got home my guy was able to calm down as well or they had forgotten about what the issue was too and they had moved on to something else.

Have Something to Look Forward To
There were times when the only thing that got me through the day was the activity I had scheduled for that evening. In my case, I had hockey and dodgeball to look forward to. This was not exciting because I loved the sports, but it allowed me to see my friends once a week and I usually came out feeling better (after pretending the puck was his face). Ok. Ok. Not all the time. But on those particularly tough days, it helped.

Find something you like to do - join a class, learn a new skill, take up playing the guitar, become an expert scrapbooker. What ever brings you some sort of joy. You might think that you don't have the time for it, but trust me, please. You will be happy that you did.

Keep a Record of their Successes
When you think you just can't take another story or demand, go to your room and read what you have written about what they have done well. Make sure you document all the amazing things they have done – that's made them feel really special and you especially proud.

For example, document something funny they said, something they have achieved, that time they were able to follow trough, had good behaviours - no matter how small. Remember your good days - don't focus on the bad ones. I think a lot of the time we are mad because day after day we don't see as much progress from our loved ones as we would like. Reminding yourself of what they have accomplished will make you feel better. You'll be able to take a step back and realize that it's just a bad day.

Plan for the Worst Hope for the Best
This is very straightforward. If you have a plan for what could go wrong, because it sometimes will, you won't be blindsided when it does. The worst won't happy every time, but at least you had a plan. This will also help you by giving you some piece of mind and your stress level manageable.

Take Five Minutes to Breath
In the article, 13 Benefits of Breathing Exercise from stressrelieftools.com, it says "when you breathe deeply, you deactivate your stress response and activate the relaxation response." This is a very key statement and so true. So,

even if you can't find an outlet at least you can do some deep breathing when your about to blow your lid.

You can go to the article by clicking on the link but in case you don't want to I'll list the benefits here:
- more oxygen in the body (blood and tissues)
- pain relief
- deep relaxation
- more stamina
- expanded lung capacity
- improved sleep
- ability to respond to stress better
- increased vitality
- feelings of well-being
- more happiness and joy in life
- clearer thinking
- improved concentration
- increased self awareness

Get Some Sleep
This is a hard job. You need to be well rested in order to handle the day-to-day vigours of dealing with this disability. Let's compare ourselves to a cell phone. If you plug your phone in at night and let it charge, it will for the most part, last all day.

However if your like me and sometimes you don't plug your phone in, your battery will only last half a day. You then are stuck looking for another power source and it could mess up the flow of your day. So, to be a sane caregiver you have to make sure your battery is charged every morning so that you can last all day long.

Laugh
Once we stop caring about the way others see you and your family, you will find these guys provide you with ample opportunity to laugh. Look for humour

in every situation, when you can. You might just find that you can turn a tense situation around in a hurry.

Here is such an example:

I had the opportunity to be a house supervisor for a young man in his early 20's. I think I mentioned before that he needed to have staff with him at all times. While one of the staff was off to get some groceries the other was left with this young man. I don't remember the exact details, but this particular staff person and the young man got into an argument. So, since the staff wanted to avoid confrontation with him, she left to take the garbage out but when the staff went outside, this sneaky young man locked the door and wouldn't let her back in. Of course I get a frantic phone call from the staff person who is very upset. I hang up with the person and call this guy and the conversation went something like this:

Me: Hey pal. How is your day going?

Guy: It's ok, I guess. I locked the staff out of the house.

Me: Oh, how come you did that?

Guy: Because we got into an argument. So, when she went outside, I locked the door because I needed time to cool off and she needed time to go F$%# herself.

Me: (trying to keep it together) Oh, and did it work?

Guy: Yeah I feel fine, but she's PISSED.

Me: (laughing so hard I'm not making any noise)

Now, I could have reacted a lot different, but the point is, he doesn't know any better. But, the even bigger point is that when your expectations are on par with the idea that it is Stage Not Age, you find yourself having a lot more giggles.

I must admit I have a bit of a hidden agenda when I speak about the importance of your health, well being and attitude. You see, I need you to be on your 'A' Game because not only do I want to make sure you feel good, but I also want to decrease the number of placements these kids have to go through.

When caregivers like you don't take time for yourself the chances of a placement breakdown increase twofold. I have worked with some of these kids who have been placed in 30, 40 even over 60 placements.

If you are on your 'A' Game, you'll have more energy and patience to deal with the challenges that come with caring for someone with this unique disability.

MAKING SENSE OF THE MADNESS

BEHIND THE SCENES

Getting a Diagnosis 63

Assessments 69

Finding Their Strengths 73

Getting Organized 75

BEHIND THE SCENES

Raising a child is like doing a sprint. Raising a child with special needs is like running a marathon. Raising a child with FASD is like running with the bulls!

Getting a Diagnosis

Getting a diagnosis is not easy. If you have been through this process, you know the trials and tribulations of having to talk to multiple doctors and collecting and gathering all sorts of information which may open a whole other can of worms if you are or are not the natural parent. But, from one article to another and from one parent to another, I am hearing and seeing that getting a confirmed diagnosis can make your experience as a caregiver a little easier.

Having a diagnosis can open doors for services and will allow you to build a more effective and knowledgeable care team for your child with FASD. I'm going to share with you some of the knowledge that has been shared with me in hopes of making the beginning of this process a little easier for you. The process might look a little different for each person, but I've compiled what I think is the most consistent bits and pieces of information that you should know about and be looking for when obtaining a diagnosis.

So, what should you look for if you suspect your child has FASD?

Well, there seems to be varying methods of diagnosis, but there also appears to be a consensus of four identifying factors that the diagnosing team will look for when assessing for FASD.

They are:

1. <u>Facial Abnormalities</u>
   - short palpebral fissures (small eyes relative to space between eyes)
   - long, smooth philtrum (area between nose and lips)
   - thin upper lip

2. <u>Problems with Growth</u>
   Children born with FASD are usually below the 10th percentile in regards to height and/or weight. Quite frankly, most babies born with FASD are underweight and tend to stay that way for most of their childhood. Folks with FASD have often been described as shorter then most and even have an "emaciated" type frame.

3. <u>Central Nervous System Abnormality</u>
   There are three indicators when assessing the CNS:
   - structural
   - neurological
   - functional

What does this really mean?
   - small brain size
   - faulty arrangement of brain cells and tissue – observable through brain imaging
   - mild to severe mental retardation
   - learning disabilities
   - poor memory

- lack of imagination or curiosity
- poor language skills
- poor problem-solving skills
- short attention span
- poor coordination
- irritability in infancy
- hyperactivity in childhood
- poor reasoning and judgment skills
- sleep and sucking disturbances in infancy

4. Maternal Alcohol Exposure

So, without adding in a ton of medical lingo, I am going to share a breakdown from The Canadian Paediatric Society that lists what these four elements of diagnostic criteria might actually look like throughout the various age stages. I find this helps when trying to picture what these signs and symptoms actually 'look like'.

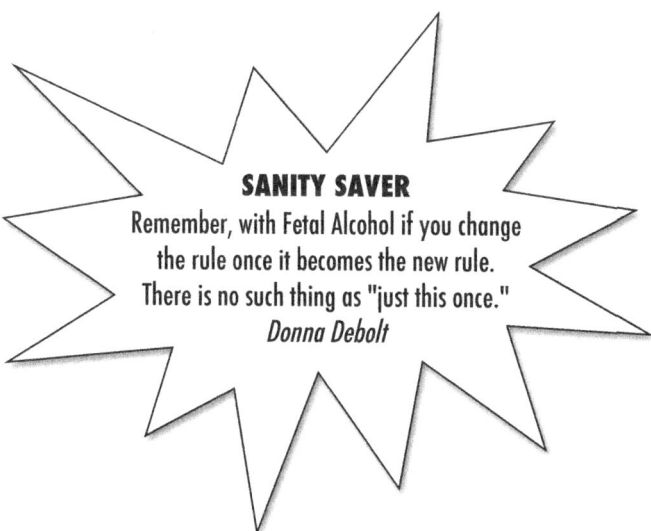

SANITY SAVER

Remember, with Fetal Alcohol if you change the rule once it becomes the new rule. There is no such thing as "just this once."
Donna Debolt

Infants
- history of prenatal alcohol exposure
- facial abnormalities
- growth retardation – height, weight, head circumference
- hypotonia, increased irritability
- jitteriness, tremulousness, weak suck
- difficulty 'habituating', getting used to stimulation

Preschool
- history of alcohol exposure, growth retardation, facial abnormalities
- friendly, talkative and alert
- temper tantrums and difficulty making transitions
- hyperactive; may be oversensitive to touch or over-stimulation
- attention deficits, developmental delays – speech, fine motor difficulties
- apparent skill levels may appear to be higher than their tested levels of ability

Middle Childhood
- history of alcohol exposure, growth retardation, facial abnormalities
- hyperactivity, attention deficit, impulsiveness
- hoor abstract thinking
- inability to foresee consequences of actions
- lack of organization and sequencing
- inability to make choices
- lack of organizational skills
- inappropriate behaviour
- overly affectionate – does not discriminate between family and strangers
- lack of inhibitions
- communication problems

- lack of social skills to make and keep friends
- unresponsive to social clues
- uses behaviour as communication
- difficulty making transitions
- academic problems – reading and mathematics
- behaviour problems – 'stretched toddler'

Adolescent and Adult
- history of alcohol exposure, growth retardation, facial abnormalities
- intelligence Quotient – average to mildly retarded with wide range; continued school difficulties
- difficulty with adaptive and living skills
- attention deficits, poor judgment, impulsivity lead to problems with employment, stable living and the law
- serious life adjustment problems – depression, alcoholism, crime, pregnancy and suicide

So, if you have noted some or many of these characteristics in the person you care for, the next step should be speaking to your doctor or another health professional about having your child assessed for FASD. But, at the same time, here are some important pieces of information that you should be considering during this crucial time. The VON Canada has compiled the feedback and advice of caregivers who have already gone through this experience. Here's what they had to say:

Start Early
The more time you have to build a stronger and more knowledgeable circle of care the better chances your loved one will have ongoing success.

Trust Your Instincts
You are the expert! You know what your love one is really like – what sets them off, what makes them happy...what makes them tick. If you are not satisfied with the response from one doctor, see another.

Diagnosis is Important at Any Age
A diagnosis is at the very least an explanation to the behaviours and can help validate that you are doing the best you can and that it is beyond your control.

Other Assessments
Consider looking into other assessments that will provide you with other valuable information regarding your child's actual level of functioning, strengths or IQ. Ask your family doctor for a referral - that would be a great place to start.

Look for a Diagnostic Team
Your family doctor is a great place to start, but consider adding other health professionals that will help you with a more holistic and thorough approach when trying to support the individual. You might look into accessing an occupational therapist, psychologist, psychiatrist and/or a family health team. Utilizing a team will bring together a variety of expertise and they will likely be able to provide you with more information about support services. The more information, the better.

Your hard work will pay off. The journey of getting a diagnosis might be lengthy but it will provide some of the answers you and your family are looking for. It will allow you to move on and provide the person with FASD proper interventions and a more supported environment. Hopefully this information will get you on your way. If you have any other specific questions about resources in your area or looking for some direction about something specific about this process, please don't hesitate to contact me at **Jeff@fasdforever.com**.

Assessments

"Getting a diagnosis of Fetal Alcohol puts you in the right city, but a good assessment puts you on the right street."
— Donna Debolt

In most cases when you get a diagnosis in the spectrum of FASD, it will come with an assessment. Understanding what valuable information is in the assessment can have a very positive impact in the life of the person with the diagnosis. It can help when you are trying to obtain services and accommodations from either the community or their school. It will help you to understand the language better, so you can "talk the talk" with other professionals.

> **A good assessment will not only test IQ and academics, but will also test the person's executive functioning.**

I have been fortunate enough to have access to dozens of assessments both through the agency I worked for and during my FASD Certificate Program (for more information, please visit www.childwelfareinstitute.torontocas.ca).

I remember the first time I went through the assessment process with my foster guy, the agency I worked for and his mother. It was a sobering experience because what we found out was that he was actually functioning a lot lower then what he was presenting. In fact, in some area's of functioning he was below the 1st percentile, which means 99% of peers his own age were functioning better then he was.

In another instance, I remember reading one assessment that said the difference between his IQ and his functioning IQ was so vast that a full IQ score would be considered meaningless. In this case, it didn't matter how high his IQ was, his deficits would outshine his smarts. Yikes!

While taking the **FASD Certificate Program**, part of our learning was to participate in consultations and I can tell you that more often then not, when there was an assessment available nobody took the time to read it or they could not understand it. I remember shaking my head when I would hear something like, 'We have to tell our client the same thing over and over. He's 11. He should be able to remember.' Then to find in the assessment that it says, ' _____ has significant short term memory issues and is found to be in the 2nd percentile'.

I also remember working with a young man at a high school when he was scheduled to have his IEP meeting and the Head of Special Ed said, 'I'm going to find out if _____ even has a learning disability.' Again, all I could do was shake my head and then point out in the assessment where it clearly said the student had significant learning difficulties and was considered to have a learning disability. What does this tell you about assessments? That tells me that they are either not read or not understood.

Jeff, I have this assessment and I don't understand it.

It can be pretty overwhelming to be handed a 200 page document filled with medical lingo that makes no sense, especially when it refers to percentiles and numbers that don't seem to help any, but only confuses you even more. If we are confused, who else is? I would bet that professionals and doctors alike are even left wondering what all the information really means sometimes.

Once the assessment is complete, make sure that you have a debrief with the professional who administered it. Then, ask them to break it down into real English. I know it sounds silly, but you must be able to break down the information in order to share it with others, so they can understand too. This is so important when we are trying to educate others!

Why is understanding what's in the assessment important?

Well, for starters, it will help you understand the strengths and weaknesses of the FASD person, so you're not smashing your head against the wall trying to figure out 'What Works'. If you know what 'stage' they are at (remember: it's stage - not age with these folks), you can better focus on their strengths and understand what their weaknesses or challenges are, so you are less frustrated. I have seen some assessments that break down the grade level they are at in each area of academics, as well as functioning. And what happens often when reviewing the assessments, is we find out that they are significantly impaired in area's that we thought they were capable in. Reading and understanding the assessment, allows me to asses my expectations of my guys. If I know what stage they are at, I am able to ask myself if I am expecting them to do too much.

And again, I believe the most important reason to have an assessment is so you can focus on their strengths. To really know where they are 'at' allows me to come up with strategies that are stage appropriate (and generally more successful).

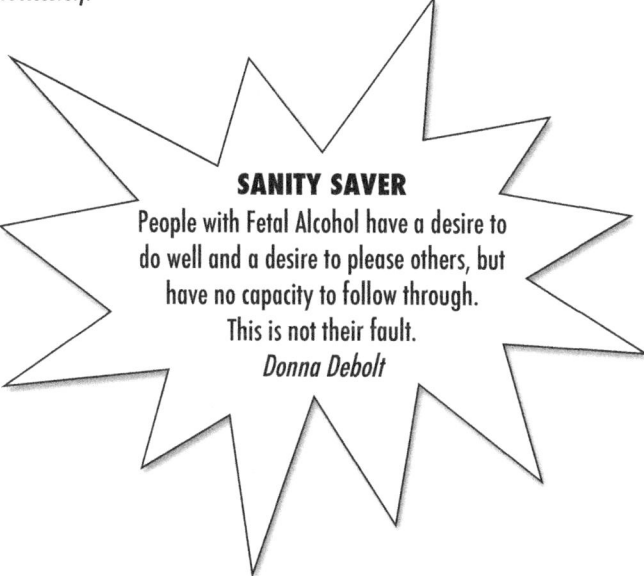

SANITY SAVER
People with Fetal Alcohol have a desire to do well and a desire to please others, but have no capacity to follow through. This is not their fault.
Donna Debolt

Example - One of the young men I was the primary caregiver for was extremely impaired in most areas of functioning. It was very difficult to communicate with him because of his low IQ and his extreme deficits with audio processing. There were so many times that he would get upset because he couldn't understand what I was saying or asking him. I knew there had to be a better way to communicate with him, so I went back to his assessment (which is painful because of the trauma this young man has faced). What I found in his assessment was there were many areas that he was considered to be below the

1st percentile, but then I spotted something that said he was in the 12th percentile in his ability to write. Hmmm, interesting.

Here is what I did with my newfound knowledge. My guy has an X-Box gaming system and with that the ability to send and receive instant messages via MSN Messenger. My phone has instant messaging. So, after a quick conversation with him he agreed to add me to his contact list. On any other day I would usually knock on his door and try and yell over the music that was blasting from his room to inform him it was time to eat, but this time I sent a text from my phone to his X-Box. Within five seconds of my sending the message, I heard the music shut off and an enthusiastic "OK JEFF! COMING!" Something simple like that changed the way we communicated even to this day. I am no longer working with the same young man, but I still get regular messages from his X-Box today. I never would have known that (or tried that) if I didn't read his assessment. UPDATE – This same young man is now sending me voice messages which I never thought he would do. I miss him, but I am sure I will see him soon.

Finding Their Strengths

The reason I do what I do is because I believe everyone has something to give, no matter what situation they are in. People living with Fetal Alcohol functioning in other area's, they CAN do a lot of things that you and I can, they just take a different road to get there. Here are some of the common strengths associated with people who are living with FASD:

- good with computers
- artistic drawing, painting, singing, dancing
- great with animals
- mechanics
- story telling (for obvious reasons)
- great with children
- fantastic sense of humour
- amazing at video games

I could go on and on but you are the expert on your child/person you know - you know what their strengths are.

Once you can find out what they like and what they are good at, you need to put your focus into that and less so into things they aren't able to do. That's why the people who know and understand this disability help people with FASD focus on life skills and not academic skills. Why?

We have to take a look at what Donna taught me about developmental trajectory.

> **A developmental trajectory describes the course of a behaviour over age or time.**

So, when we look at the living situation of the person with FASD, we need to ask, 'what is this going to look like as they get older?' 'What are they going to be doing when they are 25, 35 or 45? We need to make sure that they can have a good quality of life despite their difficulties.

So, if we know that they are horrible at math, why would we continue to expect them to learn it? All that will happen, is that they will get super frustrated and develop secondary characteristics. Also, ask yourself how much math do you really use in everyday life? Why do we have to push them to learn all of the states or provinces? How is that going to help them pay their rent or get to work on time?

If we know that they are good at mechanics at an early age the focus should be on nurturing that skill so when they get older, they could have the opportunity to work in an auto shop.

One of the families I work with, their daughter is amazing at house cleaning. The bonus is that she also really enjoys it because she is able to help her Aunt with the family cleaning business. (It's amazing to see what these folks can accomplish when they feel that sense of achievement and contribution.) Aha! The goal now is to continue to keep her interested and motivated, so when she is done school she has a real skill that she can use to help her obtain employment.

I know another young man who worked well independently with one instruction at a time. He even did better in quiet spaces. Well, say hello to working in a library! This young man was able to manage his job and even take on extra responsibilities.

What are some strengths your loved one displays? What do they like to do? What are they good at?

If you focus on what they like to do, you will find there will be less meltdowns and more enjoyment for you and them. At the end of the day, the goal is the same - you want your child, loved one or person you work with to do well and be successful. If you change your expectations and definitions of success you will find that these kids will not only hit their goal, but more often then not, they will surpass them. They will lead a long and healthy life and be a positive contributing member of society and more importantly, will keep you from losing you MIND!

Getting Organized

Appointments, meetings, case conferences – how do you remember everything? These guys meet with a lot of folks and are likely to have various people involved in their circle of care. I am going to offer you a few suggestions to keep yourself and your loved one as organized as possible to ensure that newcomers and those not familiar with FASD can get as up to speed in the shortest amount of time.

So, having some sort of tool to keep you organized is helpful for a number of reasons:

- provides easy access to all vital information, i.e. health, ID, contacts, etc.
- ensures new staff and contacts can 'catch up' quickly
- can help remind you what happened at specific appointments

When collecting information for the person living with FASD, you can be as specific as you need to be - from documenting what took place at specific appointments, frequently called numbers, criminal history, whatever you think you need at any given time.

Let me be very frank for a moment. Anne Streissguth has said that these folks are very likely to be arrested and David Boulding has said that those with FASD are more likely to plea or be found guilty when charged or arrested. This binder or whatever strategy you decide to organize the materials will be very helpful during these difficult times. Providing outside support services with a detailed history of the person with FASD can make proceedings move along faster and can even help with appropriate sentencing and most importantly, having all of these documents in one place when you need it will save you many, many sleepless nights. So, do yourself a favour and get organized, no matter how much you hate paperwork.

Jeff Noble | fasdforever.com

Where to start?
Get yourself a three ring binder and get copies of the following:
- up to date photo
- copy of health card
- copy of any other ID
- written diagnosis
- bail/probation documents
- David Boulding's article – A Lawyer's Brief**

Next, complete the following forms to put at the front of the binder. These documents are the 'quick and dirty' on your loved with FASD. **Both documents are available for download at www.fasdforever.com/madness-resources.**
- Quick and Dirty Intro
- All About Me (Created by www.kyfasd.org)

Alright. Great start!

The Quick and Dirty Intro is a really helpful tool that gives you, the person with FASD and any newcomers a very quick and brief snapshot of important demographic information, level of support and a brief list of things that your kid is awesome at. We want to share all the positives we can with people who can help!

The document, **All About Me** is a document that would actually be fun to complete with the person with FASD. This document is a little more juvenile, but very valuable information none the less. Take a look at it and adapt it if you need to for the person you know with FASD.

Ok. You now have a functional binder, or you can look at it as the life portfolio of your loved one with FASD. With all of this very important information stored in one location, it's going to help you transition between appointments and check in's with ease.

If your child or the person you live with who has FASD, requires a little more detail, consider adding the following sections or details into your binder:

- any available information or reports from school, doctors and other helping or health professionals
- statements from a teacher or teacher's aid
- detailed medication information
- comments from previous probation or corrections staff or jail records
- a document to help you remember appointments, what happened and what's next
- particular or peculiar behaviours that some folks might not understand, such as: storytelling, collecting and behaviours and things that they say that may appear as though they are more capable then they really are

Check out these templates to help remember all those pesky appointments. **All of these templates are available for download at www.fasdforever.com/madness-resources.**

- Dentist
- Doctor
- Social Worker/Case Manager
- Probation Officer
- Psychiatrist
- Family Visits

And don't forget, list all the positives you can think of because depending on why you are providing this information to people, (you may need a reminder, too), the goal is to prove to people how great these folks with FASD really are, regardless of their challenges and poor choices.

Jeff Noble | fasdforever.com

SANITY SAVER
People with FASD act their shoe size
- not their age.

Now, what else can you do to 'get organized'? The next part of this section I am going to provide you with some resources that will begin your journey and provide you with some guidance into preparing your loved one or the person you live or work with into the transition to adulthood, independent living (interdependent or semi-independent living) vocation, other supports, etc.

Remember, this is a survival guide, so we will point you in the right direction, but the real work is going to be done by you.

If you are still having a hard time connecting with these folks or getting your message across, keep reading, because the next section is chalk full of juicy strategies and tips on how to get people to listen and understand about FASD. But, first... Check these out.

Jeff's Favourite FASD Resources and Other Must Have's

- This is a list of websites and blogs that I visit frequently to keep me up to date and in the know about Fetal Alcohol.
  (www.fasdforever.com/top-10-fetal-alcohol-blogs-websites)
- FAS Community Resource Centre (www.come-over.to/FASCRC)
- Let's Talk FASD (www.von.ca/fasd)
- Finding Hope (www.findinghope.knowledge.ca)
- Disability Gerard (www.disabilityadvocategerard.com)
- National Organization on Fetal Alcohol Syndrome
  (www.nofas.org)

- The Asante Centre (www.asantecentre.org)
- Youth with FASD Transitioning Initiative Toolkit (available at www.lcfasd.com)

Housing

There are many housing options that you may want to consider for the person you know living with FASD. This may happen sooner then you expect, so you should be aware of what options are available for you and the person living with Fetal Alcohol.

There are various programs out there that offer group homes, staff supported homes, semi-independent and transitional homes. The important part to know and understand about supportive housing programs is that there are waitlists. So, if the person you know with FASD is approaching an age or is at an age where moving out the house/being removed from the house is a reality, fill out the applications and get your names on the waitlists!

There are many resources for each and every community out there, but here are some tips that you may want to consider before you start your search:

- If you have a case manager, social worker or any type of support worker working with your loved one, ask them to start researching housing options and developing a transition plan.
- If the person you know with FASD has a diagnosed mental illness, i.e. depression, anxiety, bi-polar, look into mental health housing. Often mental health housing service providers offer spots for those with a 'dual diagnosis' – a developmental disability and a mental illness – less wait times and more support...usually.
- Look beyond your immediate community. If you live in a city or town surrounded by smaller communities, check those out too. Living in a small town can have some perks – easier to build community with neighbours and other people, less busy, less chance that you will get "lost in the system". Being from a small town myself, I can say there is some truth in the statement, 'everybody knows everybody' and for someone with FASD, this could be a benefit. More people watching and being 'up in their business' means fewer chances to really get into any major trouble.

Jeff Noble | fasdforever.com

Here are some places/articles to get you started:

- Report on Supported Residential Services For Adults with Fetal Alcohol Spectrum Disorder (www.lcfasd.com)
- Canadian Association for Community Living (www.cacl.ca)
- L'Arche (www.larche.ca/en/larche)
- Affordable Housing Initiative - Information and links for low income housing. If the person with FASD is living on a low income, receives ODSP or Ontario Works, then fill out an application for low income public housing. It could be some time until their names reach the top of the list, but at least put their name on the list. (www.cmhc.ca)

Justice

If the person with FASD has not become involved with the justice system, read these articles and resources anyways. Knowing what to do or where to go before a crisis happens is the key.

- Lawyer and FASD advocate (davidboulding.com)
- FASD Learning Series (www.fasd-cmc.alberta.ca)

Education & Employment

How to keep them in school and how to find them a job!? Here are some resources to get you thinking and planning.

- Ontario Disability Support Program – Employment Supports (www.mcss.gov.on.ca)
- All-in-One Home School Resource Centre (www.come-over.to/homeschool)
- The Associated of Chief Psychologists with Ontario School Boards (www.acposb.on.ca)
- Re: Defining Success - A team approach to supporting students with FASD (www.education.alberta.ca)
- MAPS: Planning for Individual Students (www.pembrokepublishers.com)

Case Management

What the heck is Case Management? All I mean by this is get the person living with FASD some sort of 'worker'. Someone that is in a professional role that can help you navigate the system, apply for resources and/or give you the respite that you need and deserve. If you are not sure where to start, check out any services that say, 'child and family services' in their agency title, 'adult protective services' and/or 'outreach services.'

- FASLink Discussion Forum (www.faslink.org/faslink.htm)
- Developmental Services Ontario (www.dsontario.ca)

> **If you want to see success with your loved one living with Fetal Alcohol, stop trying to CHANGE their behaviour. Instead, put your focus on PREVENTING the behaviour from happening in the first place.**

Income and Financial Resources

There is a reason that folks with FASD have been referred to as 'two million dollar babies'. Here are some resources to follow up with that will help you get some financial assistance and support for you and the person with FASD.

- Ontario Disability Support Program (www.mcss.gov.on.ca)
- Ministry of Children and Youth Services (www.children.gov.on.ca)
- Person's with Disabilities Online (www.pwd-online.ca)

MAKING SENSE OF THE MADNESS

THE ART OF SALES

The Sales Pitch 85

Building Your Sales Team 95

Buying In 97

THE ART OF SALES

When people DON'T understand Fetal Alcohol everyone is mad and sad. When people DO understand Fetal Alcohol everyone is understanding and accommodating.

The Sales Pitch

Of all the feedback I have received whether it be from e-mail, Facebook, Twitter or stories I have read, one of the most common question is, 'how do I get someone to understand what the frik FASD is?' Or, 'how do we get the community to understand the ins and outs of FASD?'

Although some of us have even been there at some time, there is nothing more frustrating then dealing with people who just can't seem to grasp that for those with FASD - it's brain, not behaviour. Well, follow along because I am going to teach you how I do it - how to get people to have their own A-Ha! moment. You may have already shared this moment with someone and seen the changes take place right before you. What happens when people begin to change their thinking is that they get less angry and more understanding. But, the best part is that the folks who used to have a difficult time understanding become more accommodating; and the more people that can accommodate folks with FASD, the better the chance of your guys being successful.

Getting people to understand Fetal Alcohol Spectrum Disorder is all about SALES. Yup. That's what I said, SALES. I'll explain to you why you are actually an FASD salesperson vs. a teacher. Well, when you are trying to teach someone about FASD what actually happens is that you are trying to convince someone that it's a disability and <u>brain not behaviour</u>. All the while the person you are trying to teach is really trying to convince you, that folks with FASD are not disabled and that it's behaviour not brain. This is the Art of Sales – you are trying to convince someone to buy your product (read: understand your loved one with FASD) while they are trying convince you that your product is no good (read: bad, lazy and knows better).

To get more people to understand this disability means you might have to become a better sales person. Your task is a tough one because the fact is your product (yes, for this part of the Survival Guide, I am going to refer to the person with FASD as a product, but please bear with me) is a tough sell. However, your product does work well – people just need to understand how to use it - that is your job. Before I began my journey with Fetal Alcohol, I was in sales for about seven years. I've sold everything – from water coolers to monthly sponsorships for Fortune 500 companies. I am going to share with you some tips and tricks to get your point across, so no matter where you are – at the mall, a meeting or at the school, you'll be better prepared.

First impressions mean a lot. I wish I could tell you that this wasn't the case, but I'm just being real. When I first started in sales, I went business to business and even door to door. I was taught that I had two seconds to make a first impression. But, how the heck was I really going to? The very first thing I was taught about sales and meeting someone is, **S.E.E.**

Smile
Eye Contact
Excitement

Think about it. When you first meet a professional, a doctor or even someone on the street - if they smile, look you in the eye and were positive to deal with, aren't you more likely to smile back and feel comfortable, making it easier for your to give them the information they are looking for? Well the same applies to you when you are on the other side (trying to sell your product).

I know there may be times when you are feeling so stressed that a smile is the last thing that you want to generate, but believe me, a smile can go along way. I know I am in good shape when I smile and someone smiles back. If you meet someone and you don't smile or look someone in the eye the conversation is likely to end up being awkward and that will do nothing in terms of getting you what you want.

When I say excitement it's the same as enthusiasm. People have to 'buy' into you before they 'buy' your ideas. There are lots of situations where people have done what I have said or have my suggestions even though they did not agree with it initially. They did so, because I was enthusiastic and enthusiasm breeds enthusiasm - remember that.

> **Don't raise your voice.
> Improve your argument.**

Ok, so now that you are at the meeting and you have made a good first impression now your sitting down at a table or at a desk with a social worker teacher doctor lawyer whoever now what. Ok. Your great first impression has landed you a meeting at the (insert name of professional, office, clinic, etc.) office. If you go into this meeting unprepared your as good as done. You'll leave the meeting with your tail between your legs and that's not what we want. But you won't leave with your tail between your legs because I've got a simple formula to get you maximum results.

Small Talk
Things can be awkward if you are going to a meeting because of a crisis. So, if you need to make small talk to cut the tension a bit, but don't know what to talk about, follow this fantastic formula for small talk. Remember **F.O.R.M.**

Family - If they have pictures in their office ask who they are. People warm right up away when talking about their own family. If they don't respond they there're douche bags and you'll know
they will be a bit stiff.

Occupation - If your not at the principals office, talk about what they do for a living. People love to talk about themselves especially their work.

Recreation - What do they do outside of work? Do they play a sport you can relate to go camping?

Materials-Do they have a fancy new gadget, a new car? Start up a conversation about their possessions.

Next, **PITCH TIME!**

Chances are you have been in a position where you have had to attend a meeting because of something your loved one did or you've been in a meeting trying to prevent things from happening. Either way, the end goal is always the same – you need the other party or service to understand the disability and to agree with you about what you know are useful interventions and accommodations that work for the person with FASD. Notice I said useful, because often times the strategies that other people come with are based on behaviour modification and not brain dysfunction. In order to get your point across, you will need to have a great sales pitch.

If you are thinking, "Jeff, I don't know how to make a sales pitch!!" To that I say, "no worries, because I have another sweet formula so you can create your own sales pitch and turn those light bulbs on!"

Intro
Pretty straight forward. Tell them who you are, of course.

Don't forget - Smile, Eye Contact, and Excitement.

Short Story
Facts tell, Stories sell. The best sales people use stories to sell their products or services, so make sure when you are trying to guide people's thinking, you use as many personal stories about your experience as possible. I share my Aha! moment and I even wrote a blog post about it. In fact, it was my very first blog. I always talk about this experience - when I too, shifted my thinking from won't to can't. You can't sell someone something that you're not sold on yourself.

Presentation
This is where you present your knowledge about Fetal Alcohol and what your loved one needs and why. This is also where you present the solution. People are more apt to try things if you come to the table with a solution.

HINT: Make sure you have your presentation down before the meeting. What I mean is, KNOW what outcomes you want to have happen before the meeting.

Close Deal
This is where you ASK, ASK and ASK again for what you want - whether it be for more supports or for certain accommodations. Ask for whatever it is that you need to make it easier for you and your loved ones. You have to ask for it. Don't beat around the bush. It's ok to be blunt and to say exactly what you mean.

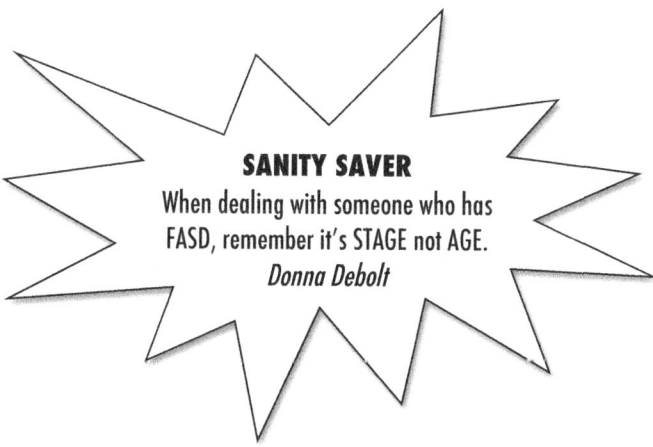

SANITY SAVER
When dealing with someone who has FASD, remember it's STAGE not AGE.
Donna Debolt

Make sure you are talking "with" people about FASD and not "at" people

This should be self-explanatory, however there a lot of times when caregivers (including myself) engage in a conversation when it starts to become more of a lecture with the other party, than it does a conversation.

What you're going to find will start to happen once you start having a conversation with people that they might not agree with what you have to say because it challenges their old way of thinking. Once you have engaged them right they will start asking you questions that go against what you are saying. In sales we call those Objections.

Objection Killing

Just like in sales, people are going to throw objections back at you about what you're saying. It's natural part of the sales process and most day to day conversations.

In fact, start to get excited when someone gives you an objection! Why? Because that means you have been able to engage them and they are going to start asking you questions because they are trying to wrap their head around what you're telling them. The problem is as caregivers we can sometimes perceive a question as a personal attack – but it is not. We have to change our thinking too, if we're really going to get through to people. So, let me teach you a few ways to handle objections.

The Feel Felt Found Method

This one is great because it's a bit softer, I think. I use this method often when I am having a casual conversation.

> **"FASD is devastating. What disability results in sufferers being good at small talk but without substance? Then add a kind heart but a violent temper, complex needs but no insight, a small frame with big expectations and perhaps worst of all, a damaged mind but a beautiful face."**
> *Elizabeth Russell*

Let me give you an example:

Let's say someone says this - *Only alcoholic mothers give birth to these kids.*

You say this - I **feel** where you're coming from, (first name - very important to use the first name...it's more personal) a lot of people have **felt** the same way, heck I even thought the same way. What studies have **found** is that almost 50% of pregnancies are unplanned. So, people continue to drink because they don't know they are even pregnant. It happens to everyday families. You can see how that makes sense right?

It's a real easy formula to follow and if used right, can be extremely effective. Let me break it down for you in some more detail.

Feel - You understand where they are coming from, like – I feel ya. Remember, it's important to understand that there are negative beliefs towards Fetal Alcohol and that's ok - make sure you acknowledge that. This method will be very effective when you relay that you understand what the other party is saying and feeling.

Felt - Say 'I felt the same way' or 'a lot of people felt the same way'. Again, you are trying to relate and make the other people or person understand that you too, used to feel like they do. You're being subtle about it, but you're letting them know you think a different way now.

Found - Here's where you can throw in a stat or a story about where you learned or got your information from. By providing this information and explaining the 'found' part of this method, you are sharing the source of your new found knowledge, making it more credible. It also shows the other party that you really know your stuff.

Remember, it takes practice to handle objections, so don't give up if you stumble a little bit at first. I also want you to make sure that you are not giving up after the first objection. If they fire another objection at you, you can also use this method:

Agree. Kill. Close.

Agree - Agree with what the other party is saying.

Kill - Use your FASD ninja skills to overcome their objection.

Close - Ask again for what you want!

I usually look to get 3 or 4 no's before I move on. Even if the meeting does not go your way this time, remember, it takes awhile for people to change their thinking. So, do not give up because there is another secret to advocating and that's the Law of Averages.

Law of Averages
The Law of Averages basically teaches salespeople that if you want to double or triple your sales, you need to double or triple the cold calls and sales presentations you make.

What that means for us caregivers is that the more calls and presentations we make, the more services we can get for the person with FASD and your family. We can't give up after one or two people say "no" or "you're on the wait list."

The law of average states that the more people we talk to, the more success we will have.

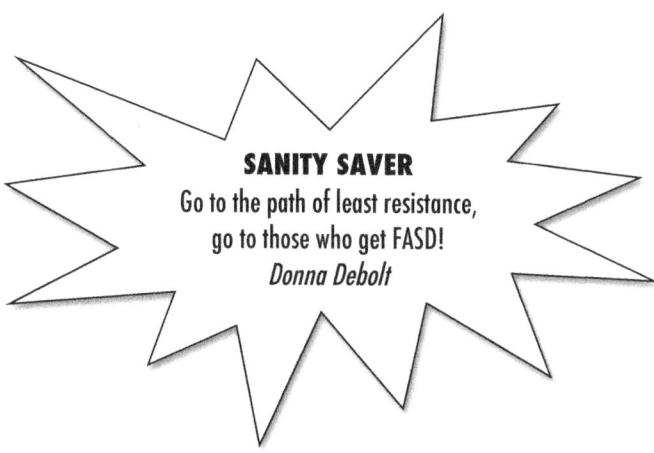

SANITY SAVER
Go to the path of least resistance, go to those who get FASD!
Donna Debolt

When I first started sales I was going door to door for a national charity and was looking for monthly donations. There were some days I would knock on what felt like one hundred doors and I would maybe get one or two sales. If my attitude was crap though, I wouldn't get any sales. That was my law of average. I eventually got better at my sales pitch and presentation and got a better law of average. My point here is that some will say yes, some won't, so what? Someone is waiting!

Now that I have given you some basic tools to start making things happen, make sure you keep in mind that when someone says "NO" to providing accommodation or supports, just remember what they are really saying is, "I don't KNOW enough about Fetal Alcohol." Don't get discouraged! You are not alone.

I know that this is all easier said then done, but it is possible. It really is. There are tons of caregivers out there who have been able to handle the same objections and the negative attitudes and eventually able to get the services they have been lobbying for. I will leave you with my performance model that I learned during my sales trainings and what I use to keep me in check when advocating gets hard.

Attitude
Make sure it's upbeat and positive - not only when you're advocating, but also

when you are at home. If you have a crappy attitude - who else do you think is going to have one?

Attitude Maintenance
It's one thing to start the day with a positive attitude, but it's a whole other thing to maintain it. If you find that your attitude is slipping during the day, have a quick timeout to regroup.

Be on Time
If you have a meeting, do your best to make sure you are on time. I know that this can be a huge issue with your guys, so make sure that the person you are meeting is aware of that before hand if you are bringing the person with FASD.

Be Prepared
No more flying by the seat of your pants! Have a plan of attack. Know your goals. Not just when advocating, but with everything you do! Know what your goals are so you have something to shoot for.

Take Control
If things are going to happen it's because you have done all the work. Don't take no for an answer.

Building a Sales Team

This is vital for your success as an FASD caregiver. Having a team available will make life for you and your loved one a heck of a lot easier. It can also give you the upper hand when you are at meetings, visits at schools or even at a soccer game. Your sales team can consist of family, friends, doctor's, teachers, therapists, social workers, police officers, other parents - anyone who 'gets' Fetal Alcohol and really understands it should be on your team. The first and most important thing you need when building your sales team though, is have a <u>Right Hand Person</u>.

This is the person you can rely on the most. It's usually a friend or a spouse that is your Numero Uno. These are the people you take to meetings with you or when you think or know you will need the extra support. It's a lot easier when you bring a friend because what often happens is you get so upset or the people at the other end of the table start using language that makes no sense, trying to intimidate you, that you forget what you wanted to say! When this happens, your right hand person should also know the plan and be able to jump right in. When you are ready and have taken a second to recheck your attitude and focus, you can jump right back in without skipping a beat.

The second reason you should have a right hand person is because a lot of times professionals may think that you are the problem. So, if you have someone with you that can back up your testimony and express that the issues you are facing are because of the organic brain damage and not the character of the person living with FASD, then you're in good shape.

My foster guys, Mom had a friend that she would bring to meetings or appointments as much as she could. Having her friend with her would make her feel more relaxed and less intimidated. Make sure you take care of your right hand person and let them know how much you appreciate the support they give you. Attitude of gratitude, right?

> **People with FASD do not want do seem like they can't meet expectations, so they will say 'no' to any plan or suggestion you come up with.**

Try and get as many people on your team as possible. The more the members you have, the more support you will get. I mean, why should you have to do this job all by yourself? Remember, climbing a mountain is a lot easier when you have someone pushing from behind and cheering you on from the top.

In closing, advocating is all about sales and building lasting relationships. If you shift your thinking to a sales approach when dealing with the challenges of getting people to understand and trying to get services, it will make the challenge a lot less daunting. Remember you can do it!

Buying In

None of this is going to work unless the person living with Fetal Alcohol 'buys in'. What do I mean by that?

For people living with FASD, feeling as though they are in control of their life (even though we are doing all the work and they get all the credit) will mean higher chances of long term success. The goal here is to make it seem cool and normal about the interventions that we, the caregiver put into place. But, what often happens is that after we do all that planning, they start to seem more capable then they really are and we hand them back all the responsibility. Well, that's where we go wrong.

As caregivers, one of our most important roles for those with FASD is to act as their external brain.

So, if they think we are babying them or perhaps making them feel incompetent, they will put the breaks on any suggestion you give them, and of course you're going to also face a massive meltdown every time you bring it up.

You can have everyone on board - social workers, doctors, teachers, whoever is on the team, but if the person living with Fetal Alcohol is not on board with the plan, disaster will follow. So, what do we do about it?

> **When people with Fetal Alcohol say they are 'bored', that may mean they don't know what to do next.**
> ***Donna Debolt***

When people living with Fetal Alcohol buy in, it makes a world of difference. When they feel like they are getting what they want and being treated like a normal person, the meltdowns start to become less frequent and they seem to be more open to help, which is what we really want. Donna Debolt didn't teach many strategies in our class, but when she did, she made sure they were ones that worked and this one works great. In fact, it's one I use all the time.

Make them think it was their idea.

This is how I do it.

Me: Hey man, remember when you said that you wanted to go to that (place) and check out (whatever).

Guy: (Not wanting to seem like he didn't forget.) Ahh yeah. What about it?

Me: I think it's a really good idea...you should do that.

Guy: (Instant chest inflation.) I know. I know. I keep telling you that's what I wanted to do, but nobody let's me do anything, etc., etc., etc., for about 10 more minutes.

Me: Ok, let me look into that then.

I know it seems simple, and it is, but it works. There are many techniques just like that one that you can use to make it seem as if the idea was theirs.

'Buying In' can take on different meanings. It doesn't always have to be about a major life decision, it can be something as simple as 'buying in' to the idea of putting visuals reminders and cues up on the walls in your home.

At first there was no way my foster guy was going to let me put up schedules and other daily reminders. I did anyway and said that they were for me, because I have ADHD. I told him, I had to put his appointments on the calendar because otherwise, I would forget. Then everyday I would have him look at the massive calendar and tell me what was going on for the day. I also had him repeat it to me because, 'my ADHD made me so forgetful'. Well, after a while this daily task became a habit. Now, I do have ADHD, but I didn't need as much prompting as he thought I did, but he 'bought in' to the idea, because it wasn't about him.

Play the Game
If we know that sometimes people living with Fetal Alcohol can't tell the difference between what's real and what's not, I'll be quite honest - I'm going to use that to my advantage and try to have them 'buy in' to what I'm selling.

Here is an example - I had the chance to work with a young man at a high school. This guy loved sports. He was really good at baseball and overall, he was pretty athletic. However, his inability to control his behaviour left a bad taste in the teacher's mouths, and they weren't convinced whether or not he should play on the sports teams. But, he loved to play baseball. So, now I had the task of making sure I kept him out of trouble and had to find a way to keep the teachers happy too.

The Jerry Maguire Method

Almost all pro athletes have an agent. An agent's job is to be the liaison between the player and the sports organization. The agent negotiates on behalf of the athlete and them they usually get compensated about 10% of the player's salary to put up with the players ego. In my case, I would be compensated with peace and quiet.

So, when I got the chance during a quiet time, I approached him with the idea. I told him that I noticed that he was a great ball player and he agreed with my assessment of his skills. I asked him if he knew what a sports agent did, and he said yes he did, and could even explain the general concept.

I explained further that if he would let me be his agent I could get him things that the "stupid teachers" wouldn't let him do. His words...not mine. I then went to his teachers and explained the concept. I told them when he wanted to ask for things to ask his agent, (me) first. They agreed. After a few days it started to work really well. It gave the teachers a relief because when he asked for things they would say, "talk to your agent" and guess what? He would!! And because of the peace and quite the teachers were getting, he would get access to the computers to play games at lunch and even got to bring some of his friends along.

Another instance is when he was having a really hard time in gym class. Instead of doing the health portion of his gym credit (because it was over his head and would have provided ample opportunity for blatant sexual comments, read - dysmaturity) we would play catch in the field. My guy thought that he was getting special privileges, but what was really happening was the school was accommodating his disability. Everyone was a winner! Don't get me wrong - every day has their challenges, but at least this made things a bit easier.

Again, these are just a few examples of what I do to get my guys to 'buy in'. You know your child the best, so you can come up with a million ways to get them to 'buy in'. It becomes fun and a good challenge. If one strategy doesn't work, keep trying! It takes practice to come up with a good story, so don't give up because you will find ones that do work. Also, let me know of any 'stories' that have worked for you. I may just try them, too. I remember Donna use to say, "it doesn't matter what you tell them...as long as it works."

MAKING SENSE OF THE MADNESS

YOUR TICKET TO SUCCESS

What Works _____ 103

What DOESN'T Work _____ 112

YOUR TICKET TO SUCCESS

The brain of a person living with Fetal Alcohol is like that light bulb in your house with a short in it. Sometimes it works perfectly and shines all day, other days it flickers on and off. Then there are those days when no matter what you do, the light is not coming on. Realizing this will allow you to react with appropriate interventions and save you a boat load of stress.

What Works

It took me a long time to figure out what I was going to say here. My goal for this guide is to give you some insight about what I have learned and experienced as a primary caregiver to someone living with Fetal Alcohol. I'm not going to sit here and give you specific strategies because your going to read them and probably tell me they won't work. Why? Because you know your loved one the best and no two people living with Fetal Alcohol are the same. NONE.

Instead, I want to give you a framework of intervention. Once you understand what appropriate interventions are, you can come up with a million strategies on your own. This is my favourite part about working with this population. So, enough of this, let's get to 'What Works' so you can come up with some amazing strategies on your OWN!!!

Environment Works
"If the work is not about the environment it's not going to work." Donna Debolt

We are never going to be able to change people living with Fetal Alcohol because we know now that their brain damage is irreversible. However, what we also know is that by changing their environment to accommodate their difficulties will decrease the challenging behaviours.

I can't begin to tell you how much of a difference this will really make. If one of my guys is in a foul mood, I always consider their environment first when trying to rule out what might be their problem. Are the lights too bright? Is the music on too loud? Are their too many people in the room? What does the room smell like? This applies to all environments - not just your home.

For example, one young man I know was so super nervous in social situations, it often stopped him from leaving the house. But, one afternoon I needed to go to the mall to get something really important. I knew though that if I tried to bring this young man in during the busy hours, it would have been a nightmare. So, I didn't even consider it because the goal is not to change him, it's to change the environment. I waited until off peak hours to go.

Less busy = Less behaviours

One of my secret weapons for environmental warfare is preparing the environment in my car. If I know my guy is going to be anxious about going somewhere, I knew at least I could make the car super comfortable for him. I always would take note of the temperature, the music and my speed.

One of my guys would always get irritated while we were driving on the highway. I couldn't figure out why and he wasn't able to tell me so he would just get madder and madder until I thought that I had better pull of the highway. Once I did that and started to drive down the regular road his behaviour did a 180. So I just kept going and took the long way.

Less attitude + Driving down a country road = Success

A few days later I was going on the same highway with a friend when he said to me, "Man, what were these guys thinking when they built this new highway?"

"What do you mean?" I asked.

He then went on to explain to me that they used different material in the concrete and there were small grooves in the road which makes small vibrations. Eureka! This is what was on his nerves. Now I knew why my man was getting so upset in the car. It also made me take into consideration that there may be things at home that were annoying him too. Sure enough! My washing machine would vibrate and make him upset as well. So, I made sure I fixed that up quick and presto - less behaviours.

When we change the environment to accommodate their disability, wonders can happen.

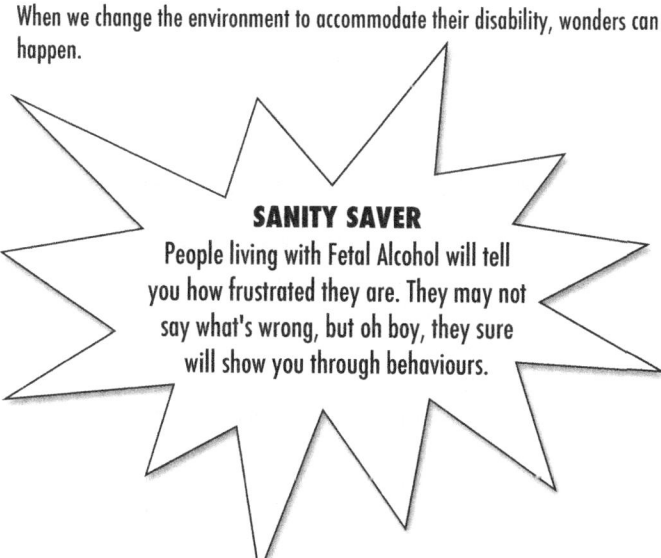

SANITY SAVER
People living with Fetal Alcohol will tell you how frustrated they are. They may not say what's wrong, but oh boy, they sure will show you through behaviours.

Jeff Noble | fasdforever.com

External Brain Works

In your travels on the internet I am sure you have been introduced to the term external brain. If not, the best way to describe it has been done by, Teresa Kellerman in her article, External Brain (www.come-over.to/FAS/externalbrain.htm). She writes, "The person who has impaired vision is given a seeing eye dog. The person with impaired hearing is given an interpreter or a hearing aid. The person who has cerebral palsy or muscular dystrophy is given braces or a wheelchair. These external devices are necessary for the person with physical impairments to be able to function to maximum potential in life."

So, people with Fetal Alcohol need someone to be their external brain so they can have support when making important choices and decisions. Because of their poor impulse control and lack of judgment, if left on their own, they are likely to make poor choices and we don't want to set them up for failure.

The External Brain should have different elements - teachers doctors, friends, mentors, even the bus driver. Anyone who the person with FASD is comfortable to ask for help from and will agree to help them work through a situation is part of their external Brain. Folks with FASD will need an External Brain to help them through various day to day tasks – waking up, getting to appointments, budgeting, hygiene, social situations, etc.

Enabling Works

It's not enabling - it's accommodating and more importantly, it works. That's why I talked earlier about picking your battles. It may look to other people like you are just giving into what they want, but you are not, you are giving them what they need. Seriously. They need that much support. Accommodating their requests will help you avoid many, many battles, which in turn gives you the peace and quiet you are looking for.

Supervision Works

If you leave someone living with Fetal Alcohol unsupervised, you are setting yourself and them up for disaster. I can't tell you how many times a crisis could have been avoided if someone was just watching. This happens because we expect people who reach a certain age to be able to behave independently or behave in a certain way. However, now that we know that impulsiveness is a direct result of their brain damage, it only makes sense that the more we are available to watch them or supervise them, the less chance they will do something silly or worse, something that gets them in some serious trouble.

> **Persons with FASD can see things in others (concrete) but they cannot see it in themselves (abstract).**
> *Donna Debolt*

I was once brought into a high school to be a Teacher's Assistant for a young man with FAS. He had an IQ in the 99th percentile for his age group and he was excellent with computers (which his peers also knew). One time, his peers bugged him to hack into the school server and shut their network down. Well, because of his impulsiveness, his vulnerability and not being able to recognize consequences, he did it and almost got expelled.

You think he would have leaned his lesson? No way. During my three months with him, he tried to do it two more times. If I wasn't there to supervise he would have been expelled from school for sure, instead I was able to intervene and avoid expulsion. I redirected him to another activity that didn't cause him to be expelled and kept him under the radar.

It's also important to know just how much supervision they really need. That's why you are the expert on your child. Don't set them up for failure by giving them unsupervised time that they aren't able to handle. Because we often do that and then get upset at them for doing something wrong.

Normalizing Works
Ok. Donna Debolt taught me this and it's helped me in many situations. We have to remember that people living with Fetal Alcohol just want to be normal. So what happens is, in our attempts to accommodate them, sometimes we can embarrass them. They don't want people to look at them like they are freaks, so I try and make every deficit they have or any accommodation I have to make, 'no biggie'.

My foster guy would sometimes make a fuss about taking medication. He would say it was stupid and that he didn't know why he had to take it. Not always, but sometimes it would even turn into a full blown meltdown. So, after learning about normalizing his challenges, the next time I had to ask him to take his medication, I set an alarm on my phone to ring while we were playing video games. When it went off, I asked him to pause the game and explained to him that I had to take my 'meds' to help with my focus and memory or I would never be able to play videogames. I ended by saying, 'no big deal'. Then I told him I would grab his 'meds' while I was up and then we could keep playing since it was so much fun. And, to my pleasure, he didn't fight me on it.

We rarely had an issue with him taking meds anymore because I was able to normalize it. Before when I would try strategies like that and told him it was for 'him', he would lose his stuff! Once I starting sharing my own challenges with him and being open about them, he didn't feel like his deficits were such a big deal. So, when he couldn't find something or if he forgot something instead of him getting frustrated, we started to learn to laugh it off.

Normalize as many situations as you can and you will see that they will become less defensive and feel better about acknowledging their weaknesses.

Bribery Works
Don't feel bad about it, make it your friend. As the caregiver, you know what motivates your guys. Most of my guys were motivated by money so a bribe that involved a sweet dollar amount to clean their room worked for them and me. But, don't expect for them to always finish the job. But, at least if I paid them a little bit of money, they would start the task.

> **Competence = Compliance**
> *Social Worker*

Habits Work
Habits are formed from doing the same thing again and again and again until we are able to do the task without thinking about it. People living with Fetal

Alcohol can learn habits, which is a good thing because it allows them to do things with out thinking about it. But, be mindful that a person with FASD will likely take way longer to form the habit and you may have to remind them again and again even once the habit has been formed. But, when they do remember their habit , it will provide them with a great sense of independence. You're not going to teach them a lesson, but you can teach them a habit.

Structure Works

Nathan Ory, a registered Psychologist does a lot of great work in the area of Fetal Alcohol and says in his article, <u>The Meaning of and the Use of Structure</u>, "In behavioural support, structure means doing the same thing, in the same order, in the same manner (with the same cues and prompts) and with the same expectations. These are the 'rules'."

So, while working with folks with FASD, I treat everyday like the movie, Groundhog Day with Bill Murray. In this movie, the same thing happens every day.

Nathan Ory makes another good point when in the same article he says, "structure of this sort 'anchors' a person. Making routines and expectations predictable, stabilizes life. It is like a sea anchor in rough weather that stabilizes a boar and prevents it from being blown totally over." Because people living with Fetal Alcohol can not see what's coming next, giving them structure provides predictability for them so they don't have to think about what's going to happen next, which will make them feel more competent.

Harm Reduction Works

Tara Says: I think this is one of the toughest concepts to grasp when working and living with these folks. Using harm reduction techniques or strategies is very simple - it's all about reducing the harm.

So basically, you are trying to achieve the best outcome of a bad situation. But, as we know these folks get themselves into some pretty precarious situations, which means we have to come up with some very interesting harm reduction strategies. This is where I would always get stuck.

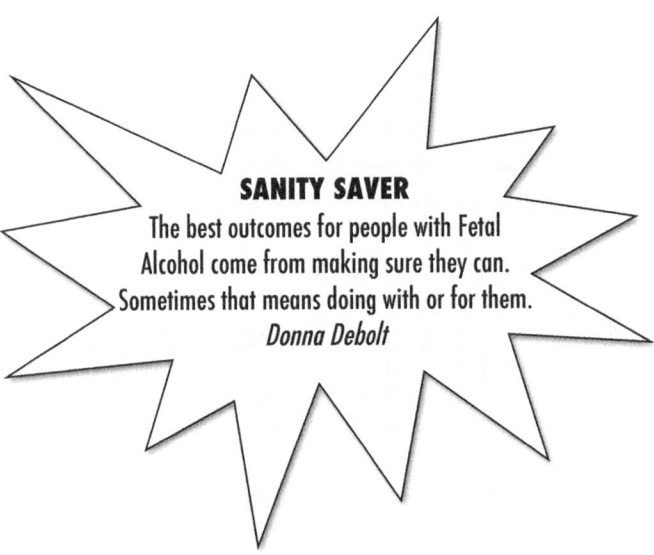

SANITY SAVER

The best outcomes for people with Fetal Alcohol come from making sure they can. Sometimes that means doing with or for them.
Donna Debolt

Let me give you an example. When we were primary caregivers, the young man we lived with was a regular marijuana smoker. So, we were often left with a major dilemma. If we don't support him in obtaining marijuana or helping him make the process as safe as possible, there is a very good chance that he could get himself in serious trouble because he would ask anyone for the substance or go anywhere to get it. He could never anticipate that he was putting himself in a dangerous situation or what the outcome could be. And then there would be the ongoing and exhausting behaviours that would develop when he wasn't able to obtain the marijuana. It felt as though we were damned if we do and damned if we don't.

I also had a really tough time with this particular situation since I am a professional who works in the field but also a caregiver of someone with FASD. So, what helped me to better understand what to do and how to effectively apply harm reduction techniques was to remind myself that these folks are going to make poor choices again and again. So, why wouldn't I want to help him stay out of trouble and to stay safe? Because I knew he was going to go looking for marijuana anyway, we began driving Clayton to the places he wanted to go. We made obtaining the substance easier and safer for him. This way, he was happy and content he had what he wanted and we knew that he was coming home safe. I know what you might be thinking, trust me. Jeff and I would debate and debate about the moral dilemma we were faced with, but at the end of the day, let's remind ourselves that the end goal with these folks is to keep them safe and alive.

Now, I am not saying to drive your kids to places to buy marijuana, this is just something that we had to do. Because in the big picture, what's worse? Him walking the streets of a large city in the GTA asking random people for pot or him smoking pot in our backyard where he was safe and out of trouble?

Individualized Behaviour Plans Work
Although there are many similarities among the spectrum of FASD, each person is very unique. What strategies work for some kids, won't for others. So, if you are raising more than one person with FASD or know more than one person with FASD, know that they will not be the same, there WILL be variations from person to person. You will have higher expectations for some folks then you do for others. I realize this is a balancing act, but it's the truth.

Jeff Noble | fasdforever.com

What DOESN'T Work

If you are reading this survival guide there is no doubt in my mind you know exactly 'What DOESN'T Work' - the problem is we continue to use these methods because of everyone's lack of understanding about this disability. Henry Ford said the definition of insanity is, "doing the same thing over and over again and expecting a different result."

'What DOESN'T Work' is very subjective because some thing's work sometimes, but for the most part the following strategies don't work **most** of the time.

Time Outs Don't Work

Time outs don't work if you are using them as a form of punishment. We use time outs because we want our guys to go and think about what they did, we want them to sit quiet and reflect on their behaviour. People living with Fetal Alcohol have a bad memory remember, so they may even forget what they are being sent to time out for - even before they get up the stairs!

When I was a boy and I had a time out, my mom would come in the room and ask me "if I had thought about what I had done?" Being able to do that requires insight, which we know people living with Fetal Alcohol don't have. So, that's why time outs just don't work. They may say that they understand and that they won't do it next time, but believe me when I say they are definitely sorry for doing whatever they did, but it probably will happen again. Not because they want to, but because they can't help it.

Having said that, if you use a timeout to help them calm down or because they are overwhelmed, that's a different story. But, please don't expect them to come up with the internal realization that they have done something 'bad'. If you use a time out as an opportunity to calm down and relax, that's good. Really good. It also gives you a chance to cool off as well. Just like a coach would use a 'time out' during a sports game - you are providing your child with an opportunity to regroup and refocus and not to punish.

What will eventually happen is they will start to build the habit of going to their room or a place where they can relax and be calm. They will start doing this automatically which is really good. They might need reminders from time to time, but they can build this habit. It also wouldn't hurt to remind them that they are not in trouble - they are just taking the opportunity to regain their composure.

Natural Consequences Don't Work
What IS a natural consequence? A natural consequence "occurs when parents do not intervene in a situation but allow the situation to teach the child. The technique is based on the adage: 'Every generation must learn that the stove is hot'."

So, if what we know about Fetal Alcohol is that these folks have a hard time putting on the breaks, have a difficult time with judgment and can't see what's going to happen next, there is a really good chance that these same folks will continue to get burned by the stove again and again - unless they have guidance and support. And, even if they learn that the stove is hot at home that doesn't mean they will know that the stove is hot at Grandma's house.

Holding them Responsible for Behaviour they CAN'T Control DOESN'T Work
Need I say more? The goal is to make sure you know what areas of their functioning they have difficulties with. For instance, as I mentioned earlier these folks have a difficult time understanding abstract concepts, i.e. money, social cues, time, laws etc. Things that they can't see.

So, if they steal something, you wouldn't punish them and say that they have to learn responsibility. Why? Because we know that people living with Fetal Alcohol don't understand what ownership is, because ownership is abstract. We would put the focus on teaching them ownership rather then punishing them because they will not learn from punishment and they will only feel worse about the whole scenario, which in turn leads to secondary disabilities. They probably already feel like crap from disappointing you, why would we want them to feel worse about something they really CAN'T control?

Logical Consequences DON'T Work
In an article I read about parenting, it said, "logical consequences teach children to accept responsibility for their mistakes and misbehaviour." People living with Fetal Alcohol have a difficult time understanding logical

consequences because they don't really understand 'cause and effect'. Because of this, they often don't even know that they did something wrong. We have to make sure they don't suffer consequences that they can't recover from.

Lectures DON'T Work
AKA 'trying to talk some sense into them'. Again, the purpose of a good lecture is to get the other party to realize what they have done, and as the 'lecturer', you might share a story or two about how you messed up and you just don't want them to end up like you did. Even if you're lecturing for good reasons, the outcome will be the same. We have to talk less and listen more.

This is also a great place to remind you that these folks are often referred to as, dysmature and they may function half of their chronological age. So, ask yourself would you lecture a seven year old about doing or not doing the dishes? Or how about getting a job? Probably not. Please remember that it's stage not age.

Taking Away Privileges DOESN'T Work
The purpose of this strategy is to take away things that they enjoy in hopes that they don't repeat the same behaviour in the future. Well, this is just silly because we end up taking things away that they like to do or play with, which are the same things that give us peace and quiet as caregivers.

The goal is to make sure that we recognize that they have a brain based disability. The focus shouldn't be on punishing the behaviours, but preventing them instead.

Tough Love Doesn't Work
This is not going to work. In fact, we might unknowingly be causing the folks that we live and work with to feel worse then they already do.

When using a strategy such as tough love, we are assuming that those with FASD will be able to control their behaviours if the stakes are high enough. But, please remember, they don't. This is why they face homelessness, eviction, bankruptcy, etc. These folks have impaired judgment and do not realize that they are making such risky decisions and choices and therefore they have no clue what the consequences are or outcome will be.

Thank you so much!

I really appreciate the fact that you took the time to read this. I can't thank you enough for your continued support of **FASDFOREVER.com** and everything I do.

If you liked the book, I would love to hear what you think about it. Shoot me an email at **Jeff@fasdforever.com**. I read each and every single comment and email, so don't be afraid to say, Hi!

Lastly, if you haven't already, you can follow me on Twitter @JeffJNoble and join in on the conversations going on right now on my Facebook Fan Page, **www.facebook.com/fetalalcoholforever.com**.

Thanks again, and I wish you nothing less than sanity!

Jeff Noble | fasdforever.com

References

Bluegrass Prevention Centre (2012). All About Me, FASD. Kentucky FASD Centre.
www.kyfasd.org/assets/downloads/AllAbou%20Me_FASD.pdf

Boulding, D.M. (2012). Fetal Alcohol and the Law. David Boulding FAS Consulting.
www.davidboulding.com/index.htm

Canadian Paediatric Society (2010). Fetal Alcohol Syndrome. Paediatr Child Health 7 (3): 161-74.

Centres for Disease Control and Prevention (2010). Fetal Alcohol Spectrum Disorders (FASDs).
www.cdc.gov/ncbddd/fasd/diagnosis.html

Changing Minds (2012). Self-Monitoring Behavior. Changing Minds.
www.changingminds.org/explanations/theories/self-monitoring.htm.

Child and Youth Services (2009). FASD101: Diagnosis and Support of FASD. Government of Alberta website.
www.fasd-cmc.alberta.ca/education-training/archived-sessions/categories/support-service-providers/fasd101-diagnosis-and-support-of-fasd/

Child and Youth Services (2009). Forensic Assessments of Youth Affected by FASD. Government of Alberta website.
www.fasd-cmc.alberta.ca/education-training/archived-sessions/categories/legal-and-justice-systems/forensic-assessments-of-youth/

Child and Youth Services (2010). Grief and Loss: Strategic Support for Clients. Government of Alberta website.
www.fasd-cmc.alberta.ca/education-training/archived-sessions/categories/support-service-providers/grief-and-loss/

Jeff Noble | fasdforever.com

Child and Youth Services (2010). Parental Expectations with an Adult Impacted by FASD. Government of Alberta website. www.fasdcmc.alberta.ca/education-training/archived-sessions/categories/affected-byfasd/parental-expectations/

Child and Youth Services (2010). The Ongoing Face of Grief and Loss and the Theory Behind It. Government of Alberta website. www.fasdcmc.alberta.ca/education-training/archived-sessions/categories/affected-byfasd/the-ongoing-face-of-grief-and-loss/

Child and Youth Services (2011). FASD: 101 - Second Edition. Government of Alberta website. www.fasd-cmc.alberta.ca/educationtraining/archived-sessions/categories/educators/fasd-101-second-edition

Child and Youth Working Group (2007). FASD: Strategies not Solutions. Edmonton: Edmonton and Area Fetal Alcohol Network. Print.

Chudley, A.E., Conry, J., Cook, J.L., Loock, C., Rosales, T., & LeBlanc, N. (2005). Fetal alcohol spectrum disorder: Canadian guidelines for diagnosis. Canadian Medical Association Journal 172 (5). www.cmaj.ca/content/172/5_suppl/S1.full

Debolt, D. (2008). Fetal Alcohol Spectrum Disorder: Considerations for Your Practice. Children's Aid Society of Toronto. Debolt. Lecture facilitated on September 24 and 25, 2008.

Debolt, D. (2009). Creating Touchstones Support to Adults with Fetal Alcohol Spectrum Disorder. Lakeland Centre for FASD.

Debolt, D. (2009). Fetal Alcohol Spectrum Disorder: Considerations for Practice. Children's Aid Society of Toronto. Debolt. Lecture facilitated on September 24 and 25, 2009.

Debolt, D. (2009). Case Management of FASD. Children's Aid Society of Toronto. Lecture facilitated on November 2009.

Debolt, D. (2009). Identification of Risk Screening for Alcohol Related Disabilities. Children's Aid Society of Toronto. Lecture facilitated on November 2009.

Dubovsky, D. (2009). FASD Learning Series: The Ongoing Face of Grief and Loss and the Theory Behind It. Government of Alberta.
www.fasdcmc.alberta.ca/education-training/archived-sessions/categories/affected-byfasd/the-ongoing-face-of-grief-and-loss/

Duquette, C., & Orders, S. (2009). Towards a Provincial Strategy: Advancing Effective Educational Practices in FASD. FASD Ontario Network of Expertise.

FAS Community Resource Center (2011). Information about Fetal Alcohol Syndrome (FAS) and Fetal Alcohol Spectrum Disorders (FASD). FAS Community Resource Center.
www.come-over.to/FASCRC/

FASD ONE Justice Committee (2012). Fetal Alcohol Spectrum Disorder & Justice. Public Health Agency of Canada and the Department of Justice - Youth Justice Policy.
www.fasdjustice.on.ca/

Flynn, Pat. (2010). eBook. The Smart Way: A Complete Guide to Publishing, Marketing and Automating a Killer eBook. San Diego: Fynndustries, 2010. Available from
www.smartpassiveincome.com/ebooks-the-smart-way.pdf

Hoy, H. & Watson, S. (2010). Oh, Those Crazy Parents! Optimizing the Service Provider-Caregiver Relationship. 2010 Alberta FASD Conference. Government of Alberta. Lecture facilitated on Tuesday, February 9, 2010.

Inman, M. (2012). The Prep. The Oatmeal. www.theoatmeal.com.

Kellerman, T. (2003). External Brain. FAS Community Resource Center.
www.come-over.to/FAS/externalbrain.htm

Kellerman, Teresa. (2006). "BEAM" Behavior Environmental Adaptation Model. Fasstar Trek Mode.

Malbin, Diane. (2007). FASD and Standard Interventions: Poor Fits? British Columbia Alternate Education Association Newsletter Summer 2005. Facets.

Malbin, Diane. (2007). Fetal Alocohol Spectrum Disorders: A Collection of Information for Parents and Professionals (2nd eds.). Portland: FASCETS. Print.

Mela, M. (2006). Accommodating the fetal alcohol spectrum disorders in the diagnostic and statistical manual of mental disorders (DSM V). The Hospital for Sick Children, 4 (23), 1-10.

Ory, Nathan. (2006). The meaning of and the use of 'structure'. Island Mental Health Support Team, 2006.

Ory, Nathan. (2007). Working with People with Challenging Behaviors (2nd eds.). Cobble Hill: Challenging Behavior Analysis & Consultation. Print.

Ritchie, B. (2007). Fetal Alcohol Spectrum Disorders (FASD) Exposure Rates, Primary and Cascade Results of In Utero Alcohol Exposure, and Incidence Markers. FASlink Fetal Alcohol Disorders Society.

Schwab, D. (2003). Fetal Alcohol Exposure: Time to Know, Time to Act. Ontario's Provincial Conference. Lecture facilitated on April 10-11, 2003.

This is Me (2007). Winnipeg: The Interagency FASD Program, the Clinic for Alcohol and Drug Exposed Children, and the FASD Youth Justice Program. Print.

VON Canada (2007). Let's Talk FASD. Ottawa: VON Canada. Print.

West, K. (2012). Natural and Logical Consequences. About.com www.childparenting.about.com/library/weekly/aa102703a.htm.

Available for Download

Article
- David Boulding – A Lawyer's Brief

Where to Start (templates):
- Quick and Dirty Intro
- All About Me

Additional Templates:
- Dentist
- Doctor
- Social Worker / Case Manager
- Probation Officer
- Psychiatrist
- Family Members

To download, visit:

www.fasdforever.com/madness-resources

Made in the USA
Middletown, DE
29 March 2024